X-PLANES 7

NORTH AMERICAN XB-70 VALKYRIE

Peter E. Davies

SERIES EDITOR TONY HOLMES

OSPREY
PUBLISHING

OSPREY PUBLISHING
Bloomsbury Publishing Plc

Kemp House, Chawley Park, Cumnor Hill, Oxford OX2 9PH, UK
29 Earlsfort Terrace, Dublin 2, Ireland
1385 Broadway, 5th Floor, New York, NY 10018, USA
Email: info@ospreypublishing.com
www.ospreypublishing.com

OSPREY is a trademark of Osprey Publishing Ltd

First published in Great Britain in 2018
Transferred to digital print in 2024

Print ISBN: 978 1 4728 2503 2
ePub: 978 1 4728 2504 9
ePDF: 978 1 4728 2505 6
XML: 978 1 4728 2506 3

Edited by Tony Holmes
Cover artwork and battlescenes by Wiek Luijken
Aircraft profiles by Adam Tooby
Index by Fionbar Lyons
Typeset by PDQ Digital Media Solutions, Bungay, UK
Printed and bound in India by Replika Press Private Ltd.

MIX
Paper from
responsible sources
FSC® C016779

The Woodland Trust
Osprey Publishing supports the Woodland Trust, the UK's leading woodland
conservation charity.

www.ospreypublishing.com
To find out more about our authors and books visit our website. Here you
will find extracts, author interviews, details of forthcoming events and the
option to sign-up for our newsletter.

Acknowledgment
I am most grateful to Terry Panopalis
for access to his extensive
photographic archive.

Front Cover
On April 12, 1966 test pilots Al White
and Joe Cotton flew the second XB-70
(62-0207) at Mach 3.08 for 20
minutes during a test flight lasting 1hr
49min, during which time they were
supersonic for a total of 1hr 17min.
The aircraft reached 72,800ft and the
airframe heated to 624°F in places.
The flight proved that cruise speeds
above Mach 3 could be sustained, fuel
permitting, and this was one of the
many contributions that the program
made towards supersonic transport
research. (Cover artwork by
Wiek Luijken)

X PLANES

CONTENTS

CHAPTER ONE

BOMBS AWAY LeMAY

Gen Curtis Emerson LeMay had a uniquely strong influence on the evolution of the heavy bomber as a strategic weapon. During World War II he helped to formulate Eighth Air Force bombing tactics, and his management of the incendiary bombing of Japan's cities was probably as decisive as the use of atomic weapons in forcing a Japanese surrender. Among his early mentors were Gen "Billy" Mitchell, who advocated the creation of an independent US Air Force based on the power of bombers to sink battleships, and Harold George, who became director of the Department of Air Tactics and Strategy in 1934 and evolved principles of precision strategic bombing that remained in use throughout the Korean and Vietnam wars and beyond.

A design competition for advanced bombers in 1935 led to the revolutionary Boeing B-17 Flying Fortress, bristling with defensive machine guns. LeMay, who became a B-17 navigator, participated in a secret demonstration of the effectiveness of bombing warships during a simulated attack on the battleship USS *Utah* (BB-31). Re-training as a Flying Fortress pilot when the US Army Air Corps expanded belatedly for World War II, LeMay soon commanded an Eighth Air Force B-17 bomb division, where he became aware of the Army Air Force's initially poor bombing results. He soon evolved the "LeMay Doctrine," which asserted that if a nation's participation in a war was inevitable it should use its full resources to win that war quickly and decisively. It was a belief that was to put him in direct conflict with Washington's management of the US Air Force (USAF) during the Vietnam War in the 1960s.

In June 1944 LeMay returned to the USA for Boeing B-29 Superfortress training. Twice as heavy as the B-17, with a 1,900-mile

Col Curtis E. LeMay congratulates a 305th Bombardment Wing (BW) B-17F crew at their Chelveston, Northamptonshire, base on June 2, 1943 after they claimed several Fw 190 fighters destroyed before they were themselves shot down and rescued from the sea. LeMay commanded the wing during its transfer from Muroc (later Edwards AFB, California) to Britain to take part in the first Eighth Air Force B-17 bombing missions of World War II. During that time he devised the "combat box formation" for the Eighth Air Force, making full use of the bombers' defensive armament. He was very aware of the inevitable cost of strategic bombing against well-defended German targets throughout the war. In April 1944 alone the Eighth Air Force lost a staggering 409 bombers, and the 305th BW lost 154 aircraft during its tour. (Imperial War Museums FRE 4378)

combat radius at an altitude in excess of 31,000ft and speeds up to 350mph, the B-29 operated above the reach of most Japanese fighters. It was deployed to the Pacific in 1944 for long-range attacks, and LeMay commanded its operations from the Marianas. After disappointing results with conventional bombing, due in part to virtually constant cloud cover over the target area, he introduced low-altitude night attacks with E-46 incendiary cluster-bombs. These wreaked havoc on wooden buildings in Japanese cities, killing more than 100,000 people in a single raid. Eventually, almost half of Japan's city areas were destroyed and up to a million people were killed. LeMay was reluctantly prepared to exact such a price to end the war.

When B-29s delivered the two nuclear weapons on Hiroshima and Nagasaki in August 1945, sparing a US invasion that had been foreseen as a fight to the last man, Gen Joseph Stilwell (in charge of US forces in the China-India-Burma theater) expressed the views of many in recognizing "the terrible military virtues of strategic bombardment." Whereas Nazi Germany had been defeated by invasion, in which air power was a vital component, the final fall of Japan had clearly been achieved mainly by bombing. The heavy bomber was firmly established as a primary weapon of war, and the doctrine that gave birth to the Valkyrie continued to evolve as technology surged ahead.

Postwar, the USAF, independent from July 1947, was quickly reduced to a fraction of its 1945 size. LeMay, as deputy chief of Air Staff for Research and Development in Washington, D.C., found Congress unwilling to fund new projects embracing fresh technology. However, even though he was known as "the big bomber guy," he found funds through the Research and Development Corporation for a missile program that utilized the skills of scientists, including many from Germany. LeMay also described to the War Department the grim concept of mutually assured destruction, a nuclear stalemate with the Soviet Union that became the basic tenet of Cold War defense, and then had to watch the air forces that could support that terrifying "deal" being steadily dismantled as Americans lost interest in defense and focused on their new-found wealth.

LeMay took over Strategic Air Command (SAC) in 1948 and found it severely run down after only two years in existence. Poor maintenance, complacency and high accident rates in its scaled-down B-29 force had diminished its credibility, and LeMay struggled to reinstate efficiency. To demonstrate the problem forcibly he instigated the "Dayton Exercise" in which the entire SAC bomber fleet was told to carry out a simultaneous, high-altitude practice radar-bombing attack on the USAF's Wright Field in Dayton, Ohio. Most of the fleet aborted before or during the mission, and no aircraft completed the exercise successfully.

LeMay's forceful personality (one journalist later dubbed him "the caveman in the jet bomber") and brilliant organizational vision resulted in a thorough shake-up of SAC, together with demands for a new generation of bombers and better conditions for his servicemen. When the North Koreans invaded South Korea in 1950, the B-29 was the only viable long-range bomber available and LeMay was obliged to provide two SAC units to support Gen Douglas MacArthur's efforts to

NAA XB-70A 62-0207

NAA XB-70A 62-0207 with its windshield in the raised position.

save South Vietnam. Most of the aircraft were pulled out of storage and only relatively small-scale attacks on transport and industrial targets were possible. LeMay reasoned that comprehensive bombing of targets in North Korea with his tried-and-tested incendiaries was the only way to stop the invasion, but US policy-makers had moved away from such drastic measures, partly to avoid exacerbating friction with China and the USSR.

SAC'S BIG BOMBER LEGACY

The B-29's successor, the huge six-engined Convair B-36 Peacemaker with a wingspan three times that of a B-17, had been proposed in 1940 as a precaution against a Nazi takeover of Britain and Europe in case retaliatory attacks from bases in the USA were required. Development problems delayed the aircraft's service entry until May 1948. The definitive B-36B/D, delivered from November 1948, could carry the 43,600lb T-12 earthquake bombs or nuclear weapons, for which it became the USAF's sole carrier. A typical bomb-load was a 47,000lb Mk 17 nuclear weapon carried over a 6,000-mile range. SAC's "long rifle" was briefly able to fly higher than intercepting fighters until the arrival of the MiG-15 in 1950, which immediately rendered the relatively slow-moving B-36 essentially obsolete.

LeMay had accepted the B-36 as the best available intercontinental bomber for SAC, but saw it (as he did all its successors) as an interim choice pending the availability of superior jet-powered heavy bombers.

It enabled him to sustain SAC's position in the defense scenario in the face of strong opposition from the US Navy, which wanted the B-36's funding allowance for a new generation of aircraft carriers equipped with nuclear bombers. US defense spending was energized by the Soviet Union's acquisition of nuclear weapons in 1949.

When President Dwight D. Eisenhower took office in 1953 he responded to the Korean hostilities and the deepening Cold War by pressing ahead with the modernization of the USAF, and SAC in particular. His priority was the nuclear deterrent, and he sought to economize on other areas of conventional warfare equipment. He believed that superiority in technological innovation would produce more economical defense solutions than maintaining large, conventional armed forces. The dominant policy of "containment" held that as long as the USA could remain ahead in technology, no other nation would risk the challenge of initiating a conflict.

LeMay became Vice Chief of the USAF in 1957, having expanded his force massively. By 1953 SAC still had B-29s, but it had added more than 180 B-36s and, crucially, 329 new Boeing B-47 Stratojet nuclear bombers, with a large fleet of supporting tanker aircraft. With six jet engines, swept wings and a top speed approaching 550mph, several versions of the 2,032 B-47s produced were retained in service from 1951 until 1965. SAC by then operated from 29 bases, all of which could attack Soviet targets with nuclear bombers kept on alert status around the clock. However, the B-47 was truly an "interim" bomber leading directly to its Boeing-built successor, the B-52 Stratofortress.

The eight-engined B-52 shared the same basic design concept but was also limited in range by the need for in-flight refueling, and it was still subsonic.

First flown in April 1952, the B-52 began to reach SAC squadrons in 1955, offering an unrefueled range of up to 10,000 miles, a maximum speed of 650mph and a service ceiling of 50,000ft. Its 70,000lb bomb-load could be carried over a tactical radius of up to 4,500 miles. Since then it has been a vital factor in "hot" wars from Vietnam to Syria, and the mainstay of SAC's Cold War deterrent posture (the Single Integrated Operation Plan, or SIOP) for nuclear and conventional bombing and guided weapons delivery at high and low altitudes.

Aware that SAC bases were vulnerable to short-notice missile or bomber attack, SAC kept several fully armed B-52s airborne at all times with in-flight refueling. This costly, but effective, strategy was replaced in the late 1960s by keeping ground-based B-52s on very short-notice nuclear alert until the Cold War situation eased in 1991. Even as the new B-52 force gathered strength, the quest for a replacement was already underway, and it seemed logical to expect another quantum leap in performance and technological innovation, including radically improved jet engines.

LeMay knew of estimates made by the USAF's Wright Air Development Center that stated advances in Soviet missile defenses would render all existing US bombers obsolete by the late 1950s. He saw this as justification for a supersonic strategic bomber force, in keeping with the prevalent "faster and higher" doctrine for military aircraft. LeMay wanted a Mach 3, long-range bomber. Planning began in the mid-1950s, when the experimental, single-seat Bell X-1 had only just exceeded Mach 2.3, and Mach 3 would not be achieved until late 1956.

When the B-52 entered service in 1955 after almost ten years of design definition, it was assumed that the bomber would be completely replaced by 1975 after 20 years of service. With frequent updates, the B-52's career is now expected to continue into the 2040s, by which time a suitable replacement should finally be available. LeMay regarded the B-52 as another in the series of "interim" bombers, and he would have been surprised to see that it remains a vital part of the US deterrent in 2018, the final production example of the 742 built having left the factory in 1962. For the low-altitude penetration mission the XB-70 would have offered little speed advantage over the B-52, and its range was shorter. B-52C-40-BO 53-400 (seen here) was one of 35 tall-tail B-52Cs, all delivered in 1956. (USAF)

Boeing had begun to research bombers with supersonic dash capability in 1950. Its MX-1022 study sketched a large subsonic aircraft that would make a supersonic dash to the target. It would be too fast for enemy radar to make a coordinated defensive reaction and too high to be reached by hostile fighters. However, this proposal was eliminated in favor of Convair proposal MX-1964, as a long-term result of which the B-47's direct replacement in the medium bomber role became the delta-wing Convair B-58A Hustler. With four podded, afterburning J79 engines, the B-58A achieved a speed of Mach 2 at 40,000ft, but it could also maintain 600mph at around 500ft. Being able to fly below radar coverage became increasingly vital for bombers as long-range Soviet surface-to-air missiles (SAMs) improved.

Although the Hustler set 19 speed records for sustained supersonic flight at altitude, its range for nuclear delivery at low altitude was limited, requiring several aerial refuelings per mission, and it was a demanding aircraft to fly. More importantly for Robert S. McNamara, who became President John F. Kennedy's Secretary of Defense from 1961, its maintenance costs were around three times those of the B-52, and its high accident rate meant that almost a quarter of the 116 examples built were lost. LeMay agreed that it was too expensive to operate and too limited in its unrefueled range and weapons load for low-altitude penetration. Robert S. McNamara satisfied the accountants by involving SAC in his multi-service F-111 fighter-bomber program, although only 76 of the planned "standardized" fleet of 263 FB-111As were provided to replace the B-58As and "tall tail" B-52C, D and F models when they had all been retired by January 1970. However, none of this addressed SAC's continuing need for a long-range heavy bomber to completely replace the B-52.

Underlying the quest for funding a B-52 replacement during the presidencies of Eisenhower and Kennedy was the increasing pressure to develop intercontinental missiles like Titan and Atlas. The gradual reduction in the size of thermonuclear warheads made this more feasible in the late 1950s. New tactical nuclear weapons, weighing around 2,000lb rather than 30,000lb like their immediate predecessors, also posed a threat to the evolution of large bombers, since they could be carried by smaller, fighter-bomber aircraft and the FB-111A.

They were also adapted for employment by submarines as part of the Polaris guided missile program, creating a major battle over finance and management of the nuclear deterrent between SAC and the US Navy. The construction of a fleet of Polaris missile submarines took a substantial portion of the defense dollars in 1958–59, with consequences for the bomber program. LeMay still considered a long-range, high-altitude bomber to be the only credible replacement for the B-52, and he strongly resisted the notion that long-range missiles had made bombers obsolete.

Attempts to formulate the new bomber were also challenged by the vexed question of a suitable powerplant for sustained supersonic performance, which became a separate USAF program affecting

NEPA

An alternative development route for powering an advanced bomber began in 1946. It would have used nuclear energy, reflecting similar developments in aircraft carrier propulsion. Very large bombers with virtually unlimited range and endurance were outlined, although President Harry S. Truman was reluctant to trust the military with management of such a risky project. However, Nuclear Energy for the Propulsion of Aircraft (NEPA) was supported by LeMay and it was intended to pave the way, via the X-6 ANP (Aircraft Nuclear Propulsion) test aircraft, for a radical swept-wing NX-2 design with nuclear power within five years.

In the X-6, a nuclear reactor and 60,000lb of radiation shielding would have been housed in a B-36-derived airframe to power four X-40 "direct cycle" jet engines mounted beneath the fuselage. Air for the engines, heated in the air-cooled R-1 reactor core or a heat exchanger, would have been passed through the engine's turbine to provide thrust. The whole P-1 installation, with a reactor operating at up to 2,000°F, initially weighed almost 170,000lb. As a forerunner to the X-6, an NB-36H bomber was equipped with a working nuclear reactor and propulsion system weighing 80 tons, with 12 tons of radiation shielding, although the reactor did not power the aircraft.

The NB-36H first flew on September 17, 1955 and made 47 flights, 21 of them with the reactor powered up to test radiation effects. Each flight was accompanied by an instrument-equipped B-50D and a C-97 transport holding a squad of US Marines who would have parachuted in to secure a crash area if the NB-36H had gone down. Although these tests showed minimal radiation risks to aircrew, the danger of radiation releases in a crash and the impossibility of preventing nuclear contamination from entering the jet efflux of a nuclear-powered turbine helped to kill the program.

Although initial tests showed the feasibility of proceeding with a second test-bed aircraft, and the Korean War had accelerated nuclear research, the Eisenhower administration canceled the X-6 in 1953 as an economy measure, although studies for an NX-2 atomic-powered bomber continued.

The Nuclear Test Aircraft NB-36H 51-5712 Convair Crusader was a conversion of a storm-damaged B-36H with a new forward fuselage. It carried the 35,000lb Aircraft Shield Test Reactor with extensive shielding and a four-ton lead barrier to protect the crew from radiation. The aircraft's escort here is a Boeing B-50, a more powerful version of the B-29. (Convair)

several projects. Typical early 1950s turbojets were incapable of providing the required performance, and they suffered from poor fuel economy. Several engines had been considered for the new bomber. Allison's J89 promised good cruise economy combined with

Bearing many similarities to North American's WS-110A and very much a part of the XB-70 story, the F-108 had a large canard and three vertical stabilizers in its first design outline. (USAF)

Convair, Boeing, and Douglas submitted proposals for swept-wing bombers with canard foreplanes and wingtip-mounted vertical stabilizers. They envisaged developments of the P-1 power installation, with four 40ft-long General Electric XMA-1A engines taking hot air from the reactor and up to six underwing J75 turbojets burning chemically enhanced fuel for a sustained supersonic dash to the target. The 450,000lb bomber might have loitered near the borders of hostile territory for five days, ready to launch long-range missiles.

LeMay liked this "split-mission" nuclear cruise/chemically powered dash project rather than the faster all-nuclear options that were presented to him, partly because the split-mission aircraft would theoretically be available when B-52 production ended in 1963. It was approved in December 1954, together with an "all-chemical" back-up proposal. The nuclear initiative was revived in December 1958 when it was thought that Russia had flown a supersonic nuclear-powered bomber, the Myasishchev M-50 "Bounder." This inaccurate intelligence, like the equally fallacious "bomber gap" reports which asserted that the USSR had vast fleets of highly capable bombers, was dispelled by U-2 reconnaissance flights, as was the similar "missile gap" myth.

In February 1955 the USAF's Air Research and Development Command issued requirements directly targeted at replacing the B-52. Weapons System 125A (WS-125A) called for a nuclear-powered aircraft, while WS-110A specified an alternative version with chemically enhanced fuel. WS-110A would have a 4,000-nautical mile range, including a 1,000-nautical mile dash with a 50,000lb load. Similar NX-2/WS-125A designs by Convair and Lockheed were given development contracts in July 1955, by which time the radius of action requirement had been reduced to 3,000 nautical miles, with a dash portion of 750 nautical miles for which supersonic speed was now demanded. Boeing and North American Aviation (NAA) chose to follow the WS-110A route, which eventually matured as the XB-70.

The launch of the Soviet Union's Sputnik 1 satellite in October 1957 gave the program new impetus, but there were increasing doubts about the feasibility of nuclear power, not least the safety factors involved. When John F. Kennedy subsequently became president, he learned of the reduced estimation of Soviet bomber development and production and duly canceled the WS-125.

The WS-110A requirement remained open, however, two-year research contracts for Boeing and NAA having been placed in 1956. They also allowed for the development of a WS-110L reconnaissance version – the normal procedure for new bomber designs, although this addition was paused in April 1956 and canceled in 1958 when CORONA reconnaissance satellites were funded instead. By then, Lockheed's U-2 had entered service, and the A-12/SR-71 reconnaissance projects for the CIA were also imminent.

a sustained supersonic dash, while the Pratt & Whitney J91 offered better sustained supersonic endurance. Wright submitted the J67 (an adapted Bristol Olympus with a separate XRJ55 afterburner unit that could be used separately as a ramjet), the key to Republic's XF-103

NAA XF-108 RAPIER

NAA's F-108 project was in many ways an integral part of the XB-70's development. As the USAF began to lose faith in Republic Aviation's too ambitious XF-103 long-range interceptor in 1955, it issued a somewhat less demanding requirement (GOR 114) for a two-seat, long-range interceptor. Although the USAF's requirement underwent frequent changes throughout 1956, in June 1957 NAA was asked for two prototypes of the F-108A, based on its NA-236 proposal. Its main purpose was to climb to 81,000ft, reach Mach 3, and fly for up to 1,000 nautical miles to intercept incoming bombers using an automated fire-control system.

Alternatively, it would cruise sub-sonically to a patrol circuit about 280 miles from its base and then loiter for up to six hours. The F-108A could then dash at Mach 3 for more than 750 miles to release its missiles at intruders. The fighter's Hughes AN/ASG-18 fire-control system would have guided three bulky AIM-47/GAR-9 Super Falcon Mach 6 missiles with nuclear or conventional warheads and a 110-mile range. AIM-9 Sidewinders were also carried on extending racks.

Theoretically, a Rapier would have to shoot down at least three bombers in five to ten minutes of combat.

The volume of fuel, engine and missile accommodation and advanced avionics required to fulfill this demanding role meant that the F-108A would have to have a very large airframe some 89ft in length, a big "cranked delta" wing spanning 57ft and an all-moving vertical stabilizer. Estimated maximum takeoff weight was at least 102,000lb. Power was to come from a pair of General Electric J93 turbojets, each developing 29,300lb of thrust in afterburner with ethyl-borane "zip" fuel and fitted with thrust reversers. These were the same engines selected for the XB-70A in parallel development with the two aircraft weapons systems by NAA. In 1958 the company even envisaged the Rapier as an escort fighter for its own XB-70A, although the range statistics were not entirely compatible. However, the company's future as the holder of the USAF's two most lucrative and advanced aircraft contracts for both SAC and Air Defense Command seemed assured. Sharing some systems and parts between the two projects would have reduced their enormous costs, and this was a factor in the awarding of the WS-110A/XB-70 contract to NAA in December 1957.

The Rapier design evolved considerably in 1958. Twin vertical stabilizers replaced the single fin, and then the single unit was reinstated with two fins above the mid-point of the wing surface. Finally, a large canard foreplane and ventral stabilizers were added, together with downward-canted outer wing panels for improved stability. Development continued through 1959, but the cost of the program caused its cancelation in September 1959. An immediate consequence of termination was a considerable increase in costs for the XB-70 program due to the removal of shared component economies.

The F-108 had evolved considerably by the time of the mock-up inspection in January 1959. A new wing planform had downward-cranked outer panels, the canard was deleted and a single vertical stabilizer was used. Two clamshell canopies covered the crew positions. (USAF)

Mach 4 all-weather interceptor program. However, both the J67 and the XF-103 were canceled in August 1957 in view of technical difficulties inherent in this extremely advanced project that proved to be insurmountable at the time due to the lack of adequate funds for their solution.

The failure of the J67 project impacted on a number of design initiatives including the XB-70A Valkyrie, but Alexander Kartveli's

CHEMICAL VALKYRIE POWER

Research began in 1954 into "chemical" power, using high-energy fuels (HEF) in a conventional turbojet for supersonic dash performance as an alternative or supplement to the ANP initiative, over which there were doubts about the potential range of its supersonic dash. Kelly Johnson at Lockheed was investigating liquid hydrogen for the CL-400 (Project Sun Tan) reconnaissance successor to his U-2, and Boeing considered it for two of its WS-110A (Model 724-16) proposals. Magnesium-based fuels were also explored.

Initiatives to find a suitable engine and fuel for the WS-110A began in earnest at Wright Field late in 1954. The Pratt & Whitney J91 and Allison J89 remained front runners, but Wright's J67 (the XF-103 powerplant) and the General Electric TF31 turbofan were also considered. So were advanced versions of the Pratt & Whitney J75 (used in the F-105 and F-106 fighters) and the General Electric J79 (for the B-58 and F-104), which was to be upgraded to 20,700lb thrust as the X275. All bar the J67 continued in development. The J91 evolved into the J58 (for the A-12/SR-71) and the X275 became the J93, which was awarded a contract in May 1958 for both the WS-110A and the XF-108A (WS-202A). The latter seemed likely to fly first. However, the enormous costs involved in the program kept constant reappraisal of the options alive through 1959, and the J91/J58 was often still seen as a viable alternative, possibly using high-energy (boron) fuel (HEF) to increase range.

Compounds of boron were known to provide more heat energy for the same volume when burned than hydrocarbon fuels normally used in aero engines. Range increases of up to 30 percent were forecast with alkylboron Project Zip (HEF) fuels, which later tests revealed as very optimistic. The belief in HEF was strong enough to persuade the US Navy, as well as the USAF, of its value for new fighter projects. The greatly increased costs and difficulty of manufacturing boron-based fuels in quantity suggested that they could be used most effectively as supplements within the engine's afterburner section during a supersonic dash, rather than serving as the sole fuel. It was also found that boron deposits produced during combustion in test-bed engines in the trials program could harm metals used for engine construction, so its use throughout a turbojet rather than only in the afterburner for a supersonic dash was inadvisable.

Furthermore, alkylboron-based fuel was also extremely toxic, requiring complex handling safety measures, and it tended to solidify in fuel lines after long periods at high temperatures.

Even so, the supposed benefits of HEF for an afterburner-only application were thought to outweigh the increased cost and complexity of the two separate fuel systems that would be needed. One would pump conventional JP4 gasoline during the cruise flight and a second would be needed to supply HEF at supersonic speed. Despite these drawbacks, the range requirements for WS-110A warranted serious investigation of boron-based fuels such as HEF-3, although they never became mandatory.

General Electric, the only contending engine company to pursue the alkylboron potential, was instructed to evaluate the fuel in Project Dash. It duly produced a modified engine, the J93-GE-5, which would include afterburner sections built with different metals or coatings to allow for boron fuel. Concerns about HEF's practicality, and the lack of funds, gradually eroded interest in the program to the point where HEF was canceled in August 1959, just eight days after a determined USAF effort to continue with its development. More than $80m of USAF and US Navy money had been allocated to build "zip" fuel processing plants, and cancelation came just as those plants were ready to start production. "Zip" was essentially a costly and hastily conceived project, and its demise reflected badly upon the B-70 project with which it was closely associated. Its loss had little effect on the technical progress of the aircraft, however.

visionary XF-103 design had innovative features including substantial proportions of titanium and steel structure and the first crew escape capsule for a US fighter – the latter concept would reappear in later designs including the F-108A and XB-70. His decision to provide the pilot with forward vision via a periscope to eliminate the drag factor of a raised canopy was ingenious but impractical, however, as was its F-104A-style downwards ejection method.

CHAPTER TWO

SERPENTS AND SPACESHIPS

In 1955 contenders for the WS-110A contract had to design a bomber that could attack military objectives, particularly airfields, within the Soviet Union from bases in the USA. It had to be ready to go within three minutes in any weather, or within 30 minutes for aircraft that were not on alert status. SAC wanted a minimum 85 percent serviceability rate for any mission and an unrefueled range of at least 4,000 miles at 60,000ft.

WS-110A was seen as likely to reach the advanced design stage over a year before the more demanding atomic WS-125A. Boeing and NAA, who were selected to produce preliminary designs in mid-1956, devised similar but highly unusual solutions to the requirements for long range with an extended supersonic dash. They outlined massive aircraft weighing 750,000lb, of which around half consisted of what the manufacturers described as "floating, disposable wing panels," causing LeMay to exclaim, "These aren't airplanes, they're three-ship formations!" as he dismissed the idea.

Each wing extension, with its own jettisonable landing gear and a full, stabilizing tail section, weighed around 190,000lb and was attached to the tips of the core aircraft's wings. Their purpose was to carry fuel for the out-bound leg of the mission, and they would be jettisoned for the supersonic dash and return flight. The idea was originated by a wartime German designer, Dr Richard Vogt, and it was

Compression lift for the XB-70, created by the arrangement of the sharp-edged splitter plate of the wedge-fronted intake box beneath the wing, was magnified by the drooped wingtips. Seen here after its fifth flight, the first XB-70 had its rear underside painted white and the intake walls unpainted. (North American)

Boeing's Model 724-13 was a March 1956 design in a series that led to the Model 724-15, the company's July 1956 offering to the USAF's Source Selection Board for the WS-110A competition. The outer, disposable, 724-1001 "floating" wingtips and integral fuel tanks each spanned 76ft and weighed 131,000lb. One of the similar NAA WS-110A proposals in 1956 included a large canard and very restricted visibility from the cockpit, which would have been remedied in theory by the installation of a periscope for the pilot. (Terry Panopalis collection)

among many advanced "parasite" solutions that included escort fighters attached to a bomber's wingtips or carried in its bomb-bay. Despite the enormous size and fuel capacity of the "formation," it still required in-flight refueling during the initial cruise flight.

Boeing's first designs included both nuclear (Model 722) and "chemical" (Model 713) studies, although the former was canceled in November 1955. Various engine options and planforms were explored, centered on an airframe 170 to 200ft long, with a swept wing spanning around 120ft. They could carry a 7,500 to 10,000lb bomb-load and defensive air-to-air missiles. The "713" series of designs offered some highly innovative sketches, including versions which resembled bigger B-52s with 12 or even 16 jet engines and twin tail-booms. When the disposable floating outer panels were introduced later in 1955 with the Model 724, fuselage length increased to 209ft, and the 118ft wingspan was extended on each side by 55ft. The outer wing tanks were 62ft long (later extended to 76ft) and eight feet in diameter. The basic airframe went through several manifestations, including the Model 724-1, which had a trapezoidal wing and no horizontal tail surfaces, pitch control being provided by a large delta canard on the 156ft fuselage.

A similarly imaginative range of ideas emerged from the NAA design offices, using floating wings with a large canard on the tip of the nose. NAA favored twin vertical stabilizers on a 700,000lb gross weight airframe that was roughly similar in dimensions to a B-52, but looking more like a *Star Wars* fighter. Both sets of proposals were rejected by LeMay in September 1956. His "three-ship formation" criticism and his observation that no existing runways could support such heavy aircraft brought an end to Phase 1 of the design process and a consequent delay of more than two years in LeMay's requested in-service date.

In re-thinking their proposals, both Boeing and NAA took advantage of advances in power and fuel efficiency for a new generation of turbojets like the General Electric X275/J93 and abandoned the split

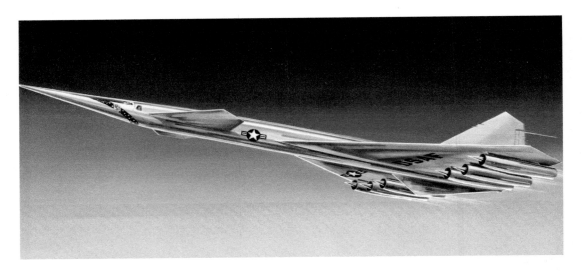

In the second design phase of the WS-110A competition in 1957, Boeing's final submission was the Model 804-4, which had evolved into a 542,000lb four-seater with upward-folding canards and six X279E turbojets under a trapezoidal wing. Its fuselage measured 208.6ft and it would have carried a single 25,000lb bomb. (Terry Panopalis collection)

mission and floating wing concept in favor of aircraft that could cruise at supersonic speed. A new USAF request was issued in September 1957 for an aircraft capable of cruising at Mach 3 and 70,000–75,000ft, with a 10,500-nautical mile range. The two companies were given only 45 days to offer proposals, and the outcomes generally resembled the "core" aircraft from Phase 1, but with six engines – podded in the case of Boeing's Model 804 and internally mounted in NAA's drawings. Boeing still favored a single vertical stabilizer, a trapezoidal wing, and forward vision, at low speed only, through small slit windows.

In 1957 NAA designers Alfred Eggers and Clarence Syverston became aware of an aerodynamic phenomenon known as compression lift, expounded by two National Advisory Committee for Aeronautics (NACA) scientists in a 1956 report. NACA found that the greatly increased aerodynamic drag at supersonic speeds could be reduced by using the area of high air pressure created beneath the aircraft and behind the shockwave that it generated by moving at supersonic speed. By using a large, wedge-fronted box-like air intake structure for the engines, a high-pressure zone could be created, and since this was not matched by an equivalent pressure area above the wing, lift could be increased by up to a third, significantly increasing the aircraft's range as it "surfed" on its own shockwave. This discovery influenced the NAA design considerably and helped to create the distinctive appearance of the XB-70.

A large, wedge-fronted section containing the air intakes and six engines was situated beneath a massive delta wing and twin vertical stabilizers. The intake box, echoing the wing's delta format, was designed to reduce airflow to around Mach 1.3 ahead of the engines when the aircraft itself was traveling at Mach 3. Excess air was expelled through bypass doors. The fuselage extended forward from above the wing in what became a distinctive cobra-like profile and a delta canard was situated above and behind the cockpit. The wingtips could be folded downwards at supersonic speeds to add stability. It was found that this wing configuration also increased the compression lift effect,

The center fuselage section of XB-70 AV1 is moved into position to join with the forward fuselage. This stainless steel structure was an integral fuel tank for part of the aircraft's massive fuel load of around 50,000 gallons, which acted as a useful heat sink at high speeds. Careful checks on the fuel distribution system and tank contents gauges were a primary task after the roll-out of AV1. It was found that fuel economy at the aircraft's maximum speed was up to twice as good as the consumption figures at subsonic speeds. Although the engines used twice as much fuel, the aircraft was covering four times the distance that it would fly at subsonic speeds. Completing most of the mission at Mach 3 therefore became more practical than making a supersonic dash. (North American)

a crucial factor in the NAA design's eventual success and an asset in the effort to compensate for the increased weight and fuel load required for prolonged supersonic flight. Boeing did not attach much credibility to compression lift.

DECISION TIME

Both WS-110A Chemically Powered Bomber proposals were thoroughly evaluated by the USAF's Source Selection Board in October and November 1957, and the NAA offering emerged as the clear favorite for the 60-man evaluation team when their decision was revealed on December 23. The company had a long track record of supplying the USAF with outstanding aircraft such as the P-51 Mustang and F-86 Sabre, making it the biggest US military defense contractor on several occasions during the 1950s. NAA's XSM-64A Navaho was its most lucrative contract in that decade in respect to technical innovation, this pilotless supersonic bomber/cruise missile being designed to achieve Mach 3 at 77,000ft while covering a distance of 3,500 nautical miles. Powered by ramjets and large rocket boosters, it relied on NAA's Autonetics division for its newly developed inertial guidance system and the company's Rocketdyne division for its liquid-fuel rocket boosters.

Although Navaho was canceled in 1957 in favor of long-range missiles, the Rocketdyne engines were used for the Atlas intercontinental ballistic missile (ICBM), thus allowing NAA to partly recoup the huge investment it had made in the abandoned project. The company also gained experience in using metals such as titanium for the heat-resistant components that were needed for high supersonic speeds. Its 1953 X-10 jet-powered, Mach 2 pilotless research craft, built to test Navaho technology, also provided experience of the aerodynamics of the canard that would reappear in the XB-70 proposals.

Boeing's traditional role as supplier of heavy bombers to the USAF prompted the company to demand a congressional inquiry into the choice of NAA's WS-110A, but the decision was upheld. Boeing became sub-contractors to NAA (the overall weapons system contractors), producing the B-70 wings, while other sections of the production task were spread widely among a range of companies across the USA. Lockheed was awarded the aft fuselage contract, Chance-Vought the tail and flying control surfaces, General Electric produced the electronic countermeasures (ECM) equipment, and hundreds of companies including Motorola, IBM, Autonetics, Sundstrand, John Oster, AiResearch, and others shared component manufacture. All the contracts were subject to fierce bidding, with no fewer than 21 companies competing for the construction of the vertical tails alone. When the whole program seemed on the verge of cancellation in 1958–59 Boeing handed the wings contract back to NAA, preferring to use its production space for commercial aircraft.

NAA's program would be overseen by Raymond H. Rice (lead designer of the F-86 Sabre and F-100 Super Sabre) at the company's Los Angeles division under the supervision of James "Dutch" Kindelberger, its founder and chairman. Much of the initial negotiation over the design had fallen to Harrison Storms, whose main focus at the time was increasingly on the X-15 research rocket aircraft (see Osprey X-Planes No. 3 – *North American X-15* for further details). Rice estimated that up to 20,000 companies would have benefited from B-70 production work.

The importance of strategic bombers alongside missiles was emphasized in a contemporary Air Research and Development Command (ARDC) report. Missiles could only be targeted on "unhardened, accurately located targets [particularly cities or fixed military bases]. Such targets comprise only part of the strategic target system." Bombers were still required for "smaller targets, some of which may be hardened to the extent that they can only be destroyed by accurate bombing with high yield weapons. For such tasks a manned bomber is the only known system possessing the needed and proven capabilities."

ARDC also asserted that, in an age of increasing automation, it was still important to have a human presence to deal with malfunctions, sudden changes of plan or last-minute revisions of target and other issues that were beyond the capability of long-range nuclear missiles. Additionally, it stated that bombers gave the flexibility to cope with more limited conflicts using less destructive weapons, or merely to act as psychological deterrents by their appearance over potential trouble spots. Although such views seemed to be at odds with the prevalent thinking of the Eisenhower administration, they showed clear foresight in understanding the shortcomings of unmanned attack systems, and fortuitously anticipated the actual uses of bombers in the following

XB-70 COCKPIT

1. Visor heater rheostat
2. Control system power augmentation switches
3. Ground escape hatch jettison handle
4. Pilot's control wheel
5. Primary pitch trim knob
6. Pilot's air outlet
7. Adjustable air outlet
8. Rudder pedal adjustment knob
9. Airspeed/Mach number indicator
10. Attitude director indicator
11. Altitude vertical velocity indicator
12. Horizontal situation indicator
13. Total temperature gauge
14. Sideslip indicator
15. Engine/gearbox vibration indicators
16. Encapsulate caution light switch
17. Standby attitude indicator
18. Bail-out warning light button
19. Standby altimeter
20. Pilot's seat and encapsulation/ejection controls
21. Cabin pressure altimeter

22. Ammonia quantity gauge
23. Liquid oxygen quantity gauge
24. AC voltmeter bus selector
25. Standby gyro fast erect button
26. Electronic compartment air temperature gauge
27. Water quantity gauge
28. Correlation counters and instruments
29. Fire warning and engine shutdown lights (x6)
30. Tachometers (x6)
31. Exhaust temperature gauges (x6)
32. Primary exhaust nozzle position indicators (x6)
33. Hydraulic reservoir indicators and switches
34. Landing gear handles and position lights
35. Primary and utility hydraulic pressure gauges
36. Wingtip position selector and indicators
37. Throttles (x6)
38. Alternate throttle switches (x6)

39. UHF control panel
40. Flight augmentation and trim control panel
41. ILS controls
42. Pilot's intercom panel
43. Co-pilot's intercom panel
44. Nosewheel steering controls
45. Flap handle
46. Air inlet shockwave and throat Mach schedule indicators (left and right)
47. Air inlet pressure ratio gauges (left and right)
48. Air inlet control system panel
49. Fuel tank sequence indicator
50. Fuel tank pump switches
51. Co-pilot's attitude, altitude and speed indicators (similar to pilot's)
52. Total fuel quantity indicators
53. Controls for inlet system
54. Co-pilot's control column (similar to pilot's)
55. Co-pilot's seat

decades. LeMay's successor as Commander-in-Chief of SAC in July 1957, Gen Thomas Power, endorsed this concept of a mixed bomber and missile force, with the US Navy's missile-launching submarines as the other main component.

By January 1958 WS-110A's intended mission requirements had become clearer, and there were some additions, including a requirement for low-altitude bombing prompted by improvements in potentially hostile radar defense and ground-to-air missile networks. It was clear that the B-70 design would be unsuited to low-altitude penetration without considerable modification, or the use of a variable geometry "swing-wing" configuration. The revised speed parameters were Mach 3 at high altitudes up to 75,000ft, and a high subsonic speed for penetration at low altitude, carrying up to 20,000lb of "special" (nuclear) weapons. Allowance was also made for a load of smaller ordnance, or stand-off guided weapons with a range of up to 700 nautical miles, and these, together with provision for external fuel tanks, were included in alterations to the specification early in 1959 that made the aircraft a Missile Platform Bomber. Some of the larger missiles, such as Skybolt, would probably have been carried on underwing pylons.

Early plans around the time of WS-110A also called for self-defense missiles in addition to on-board ECM installations. Rearward-firing air-to-air missiles might have been installed in a rotary launcher in the rear fuselage. Some of them, or a rotary cannon, could have been loaded with pellets to create a cloud of destructive fragments that would destroy or deflect enemy missiles, or damage them with corrosive chemical substances. These projects had been closed down by mid-1959. Another futuristic initiative at that time was Project Pye Wacket. Up to ten 510lb missiles shaped like flying saucers would have been released, and each had an infrared seeker that could be directed towards an incoming target up to 75 miles away via a radio link between the bomber and its own autopilot. The missile would then have been propelled by two rocket motors on an interception course to destroy a fighter with its 50lb warhead.

Contracts were signed on January 24, 1958, and the project became the B-70 the following month, with the official name Valkyrie applied in July 1958 after a USAF competition in which TSgt Francis Seller suggested the legendary Norse title in one of more than 20,200 entries. He was one of 12 to suggest that name. "Valkyrja," who were mythical, beautiful female warriors dressed in white robes, were the "choosers of the slain" who decided which soldiers killed in battle deserved to be taken to Valhalla to serve the god Odin. They rode the clouds on their battle-chargers, clad in armor and hurling lightning bolts at their enemies.

The aircraft was to have an in-service date of late 1965 for the first SAC wing, two years after LeMay's original deadline. Two months later, in March 1958, the demands were tightened, the program was accelerated, and the operational in-service date was moved forward to August 1964. Performance increases now required a maximum altitude of 80,000ft and a range of 6,873 nautical miles. Creating the XB-70 had become one of the most demanding tasks expected of the aviation industry, and it also aroused unprecedented levels of political controversy. Many critics increasingly argued that such high performance, achieved at massive expense, was no longer a guarantee of reaching a target intact.

Uncertainty also continued over the engine for the new bomber, partly due to continued indecision about the "zip" fuel project that would persist for another year. The Pratt & Whitney J58 was again briefly considered, but full backing was given to General Electric's promising J93 instead. It was agreed that the YJ93-GE-3 version would be used for both the F-108 fighter and XB-70, while the HEF-3 boron-fueled J93-GE-5 version continued in development.

DESIGN DEFINITION

With a critical deadline now before them, NAA designers worked on the details of their ground-breaking challenge, making many changes during 1958. By the end of the year the cockpit windshield, which was at first a fixed set of transparencies, was given a moveable ramp which was raised to streamline the nose and reduce supersonic drag. The canard, which was subjected to many hours of wind-tunnel testing, went through several configurations that took it from being a relatively large delta at the top of the fuselage through several mid-wing positions to a smaller shape behind the cockpit.

As the year progressed a second 14ft-long weapons bay was added at the expense of two internal fuel tanks, and the pessimistic forecasts concerning "zip" fuel resulted in a decision to accommodate a "dual fuel" feature with additional standard JP-4 fuel to meet the range parameters. These changes added 54,000lb to the gross weight, and necessitated revision of the undercarriage. By December the airframe plans were revised to increase the area of the folding outer wing panels by moving the fold-line inwards by one fifth. The twin vertical stabilizers were reduced in area since the hinged wing panels gave added stability, and they became all-moving without rudders. The fuselage was increased in volume aft of the intake "wedge" and given a smoother continuous profile from nose to tail. In December 1958 drawings of the flying control surfaces were also modified to allow for five elevons (combined ailerons and elevators) per wing instead of three. With these changes approved, a mock-up with the fake "buzz" number "BX-000" on its fuselage was built and reviewed by April 4, 1959.

The overall design effort was greatly assisted from the outset by the research into high-Mach flight and aircraft structures that had been undertaken throughout the 1950s by the USAF and NACA (National Aeronautics and Space Administration – NASA – after 1958). Aircraft such as the Bell X-1 (see Osprey X-Planes No. 1 – *Bell X-1* for further details), X-2 (see Osprey X-Planes No. 6 – *Bell X-2* for further details), and Douglas D-558 had provided vital data, and NAA's own X-15 hypersonic research aircraft was approaching its first flight in 1959. The latter would eventually provide a wealth of data for high-Mach engineering, but it was mainly of use in designing air vehicles that would greatly exceed the XB-70's speed.

HOT AND COLD

President Eisenhower had always doubted the necessity of the sophisticated B-70, and he increasingly shared the prevalent belief that long-range missiles had made the bomber redundant – a view that was enthusiastically promoted by the missile manufacturers and overstated by the President to stir up debate. He

A YJ93-GE-3 from the No. 2 engine bay on AV1. Despite their size, the policy of attaching engine accessories to the airframe rather than the engine itself simplified changing an engine and reduced the time needed for this task to around 25 minutes. (North American)

doubted that the B-70 would be in service before 1969, by which time missiles would have been perfected and Soviet defenses would have made the bomber too vulnerable in his estimation. By resisting the allocation of extra funds in 1958 he stopped the accelerated program to bring the B-70 into service use by August 1964. He also recommended that, having already received more than $350m of development support money, the XB-70 prototype should demonstrate its advertised performance before it received full funding. However, Eisenhower did sign the Fiscal 1960 budget, which included increased provision for the F-108 and B-70 as the two principal types to be developed in that period.

Throughout January 1959 the debate about engine choices continued. Pratt & Whitney's J58 was still favored by some Pentagon advisors, but the General Electric YJ93 had the potential advantage of using an HEF-powered afterburner, and it was still seen as the powerplant for both the B-70 and F-108 as an economy factor. The cancelation of the HEF program, which inevitably killed the J93-GE-5, was in many ways the first stage in the Valkyrie's gradual demise. With commendable foresight, NAA had already made contingency allowances in the design to try and preserve the bomber's range in other ways, and compensate for the ten percent reduction (and three percent thrust reduction) without HEF. Omitting the extra fuel system equipment needed to provide dual fuel capability saved weight and progressive refinement of the B-70 airframe with wind-tunnel models also helped to preserve the aircraft's endurance and range.

Also, the USAF had sought more efficient jet fuels since 1956 as an alternative for its F-108 and WS-110A. The result was JP-6, a more stable derivative of the US Navy's JP-5. The rival J58 engine required a more sophisticated JP-7 version, which was optimized for high-altitude performance at low temperatures and eventually produced only for the J58-powered Lockheed SR-71. Cancelation of HEF boron fuel refocused attention on JP-6, and it appeared that a slightly modified YJ93-GE-3 would meet the requirements on range, rate of climb, and altitude in most respects, using JP-6 without the safety problems and

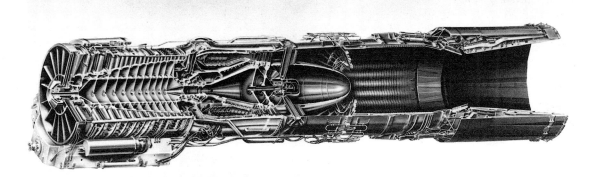

The interior structure of the General Electric YJ93-GE-3, the chosen power source for the XB-70 and F-108. A thrust reverser was designed for the fighter version. Its performance, with maximum afterburning thrust of 29,300lb and a Mach 3.2 speed limit, was a spectacular achievement in 1957. (GE/Terry Panopalis collection)

extra weight associated with an HEF engine. The cancelation of the F-108 on September 24, 1959 was a much more serious setback, adding around $180m to B-70 development costs and providing ammunition for its growing number of critics.

In his final year as president, Eisenhower was no more enthusiastic about the B-70, and his antipathy to the bomber was echoed by many in his Administration and particularly by his budget director, Maurice Stans, who was seeking drastic cuts and strongly favored the missile lobby at the Pentagon. The Atlas and Titan ICBM programs had already absorbed $3bn of USAF money, and the even more costly Minuteman missile was about to be produced. While loss of faith in the B-70 was a blow to the established belief that American technical dominance should be maintained at almost any cost, it also seemed that, with the B-70, that cost had finally become too great.

Cancelation seemed likely but the outcome on December 1, 1959 was severe limitation on funding the project, culminating in reduction of the whole program to a single XB-70 prototype and a few of its relevant systems such as the IBM bombing and navigation computer. The sole example was scheduled to conduct a flight-test program from 1963 to 1967, taking the responsibility for its fate into another presidency.

For Scott Crossfield, NAA's pilot for the company's X-15 test flights, the cuts were a stunning shock, coming so soon after the loss of the F-108. "North American would build one prototype, a gutless shell with no armament or weapons system." All the major sub-contracts were canceled. The company was apparently going to build one XB-70 on the same research vehicle basis as the X-15 – a venture which it had initially rejected for being non-profit-making. The cut-back was seen as the prelude to complete cancelation as a USAF requirement, leaving NAA with only a few T-39 executive jets on its production lines. To Crossfield, "The last of the manned airplanes was all but gone."

The USAF's response to this drastic blow was immediate. The Joint Chiefs of Staff Chairman, Gen Nathan Twining and Lt Gen Bernard Schriever, head of ARDC, emphasized to Congress the flexibility of bombers compared with missiles. Curtis LeMay had already alienated the Senate Majority Leader, Lyndon B. Johnson (later to be president),

The wing-less AV1 being moved to the final assembly stage at Palmdale. The fixed sections of the vertical stabilizers are in place and await the moveable rudders. (Terry Panopalis Collection)

in 1957 in a dispute over USAF pay, and he found few allies in either house for his defense of the bomber program. Although Eisenhower had been a distinguished military leader, he saw the late 1950s as a time of relative stability and inaction in the Cold War, coupled with excessive defense expenditure. This in turn meant that he saw no requirement for hugely expensive ventures like the B-70. Many in Congress and the Pentagon agreed with Eisenhower. This policy would be partially reversed by his successor, John F. Kennedy, however.

Gen Thomas White, USAF Chief of Staff, echoed ARDC's view that the flexibility of a bomber was vital at a time when the ICBM was still very much an untested weapon that offered only one option, and could not be recalled. ICBMs could have been unstoppable by existing defenses, but that applied to both sides. SAC's established "positive control" procedure would require nuclear-armed B-70s to take off under Presidential authority when there was credible warning of an attack, but they could be recalled during their flight and would head home in any case if they did not receive the "go code" signal to continue with the attack. On receipt of that ominous command, nuclear weapons would be armed in a complex sequence of actions involving more than one crew member. Implicit in that situation was the assumption that nuclear weapons would already have fallen on US territory. ICBMs were not seen to be capable of such flexible control, so the idea of widening the options by establishing a mixed force of ICBMs, B-70s, and B-52s, with submarine-launched missiles for a "second strike" follow-up attack, gained currency in Congress.

A very complex access structure had to be built for the final assembly of AV1, including the attachment of the wings. NAA pioneered the use of chemical milling of titanium parts, having already gained experience with the use of titanium and aluminum honeycomb sandwich structures in the pioneering methods the company had developed to manufacture its F-100 Super Sabre in the 1950s. In 1953 NAA used 95 percent of the titanium alloy made in America. (North American)

The efforts of Gen White and Lt Gen Roscoe Wilson (Deputy Chief of Staff, Development) were instrumental in adding another $75m to the $365m allowed in the FY 1961 budget to build the prototype XB-70, followed by 12 development B-70s. A supplementary contract issued on September 21, 1960 (bringing overall costs to $1.3bn) funded a second XB-70 and a single YB-70 operational development example. The first three aircraft became known in NAA as AV (air vehicle) 1, 2, and 3, with the USAF serials 62-0001, 62-0207, and 62-0208. The YB-70 (AV3) would also have tested a prototype of the bombing-navigation system. Eisenhower still believed that the B-52 was adequate for foreseeable needs, and that it would shortly be replaced by missiles, but in the last months of his presidency he had at least kept the B-70 project alive, and agreed in principle to 12 development aircraft.

VALKYRIE VERSUS THE ACCOUNTANTS

The inauguration of President John F. Kennedy in 1961 brought very different approaches to defense issues. He had judiciously supported the allocation of new funding for the B-70 project in November 1960, saying "I endorse wholeheartedly the B-70 manned aircraft." Renewed interest in the project's feasibility after a lengthy revaluation, and a realization that Soviet antiaircraft missile development had been slower than anticipated, had resulted in the B-70 being "restored to full weapon-system status" in an August 1, 1960 contract. In retrospect this was derived partly from a vote-seeking, pre-election pledge by both political parties who were aware of the continued national interest in the B-70 as a lucrative job-creator. The 12-aircraft contract was also reinstated in September, and several of the crucial sub-contracts for electronic components had been revived by November.

However, Kennedy's Secretary of Defense, Robert S. McNamara (who had previously worked for LeMay in the USAAF Office of Statistical Control, and often found fault with the general's accountancy procedures), imported a team of "defense intellectuals" who lacked military experience and were reluctant to take advice from military leaders. There would be many reasons to doubt their self-assurance. For example, warnings from generals, including LeMay, that the Bay of Pigs invasion of Cuba in April 1961 was doomed were ignored, with disastrous consequences. Their policies were shaped by statistical analysis of problems, using data which could be processed to fit in with their requirements.

They also resisted radical innovation in technology, and the WS-110A was a prime example of that. Cost-effectiveness became the inflexible rule for defense procurement rather than considered evaluation of the needs of the armed services. McNamara, who had accepted the role of Secretary of Defense only on condition that he would have complete control of his department, perpetuated the Eisenhower administration's belief that bombers should give way to cheaper missiles, adding that new programs should be shared between the three armed forces to save money. He wanted "one defense policy, not three conflicting defense policies." For LeMay, who Kennedy appointed Chief of the USAF in 1961 despite his obvious opposition to McNamara's influence, there were new struggles ahead, and the WS-110A bomber was central to many of them.

When Kennedy took office it was clear to his advisors that little tangible progress had actually been achieved with the XB-70 despite the expenditure of more than $1bn in the previous 15 years. The ANP program was finally canceled in March 1961, and within months of Kennedy's arrival McNamara was asserting that missiles "make unnecessary and economically unjustifiable the development of the B-70 as a full weapon system." The program would be supported only for research into Mach 3 flight with "an airframe potentially useful as a bomber," together with its "related bombing and navigation systems," but, from March 31, 1961, only three aircraft were to be produced. McNamara then canceled the previously agreed batch of 12 B-70As (including the YB-70A) in April 1961, and on July 31 the $395m approved for the project was reduced to only $75m. Development of the IBM bombing-navigation system was to continue, however, as it could have wider uses.

Underlying this decision were several further changes in the wider perception of the manned, high-altitude bomber. A primary consideration was the unexpectedly effective performance of the SA-2 "Guideline" SAM in shooting down Gary Powers' U-2 in May 1960. The generally disorganized way in which that interception took place was not known for many years, but the immediate revelation of the missile's capability was a salutary lesson that would begin to have devastating consequences for US air power in the Vietnam War five years later. Although powerful ECM equipment was developed to protect bombers like the B-52, it was recognized that SAMs fired in salvoes would eventually find their mark by sheer force of numbers.

It was also learned that the Soviet Union was developing the MiG-25 "Foxbat" – a crude but effective supersonic fighter specifically designed to intercept the U-2 and other high flyers such as the XB-70. Although it did not fly until 1964, the MiG-25 was the culmination of a series of Soviet high-altitude interceptor developments, including the MiG-21,

The variable-position outer windshield ramp could be operated at most points in the flight envelope, and it could be lowered for a "quick look" at high speed if necessary. The cockpit side windows were used for old-fashioned "eyeball-powered" location of landmarks since the TACAN and other electronic means of navigation were sometimes unreliable. (North American)

begun in the 1950s in response to the appearance of the B-52 and the seemingly imminent B-70. Constructed mainly of stainless steel, it was known to be capable of achieving Mach 3 and ceilings of up to 89,000ft thanks to the immense power – around 50,000lb – produced by its two Tumansky R-15 turbojets. Although the MiG-25's range was limited to 935 nautical miles, its R-40 guided missiles were a threat to any high-flying intruder.

Such strong opposition forced USAF strategists to develop the B-52G/H Stratofortress's stand-off missile-launching role, and also to look for a new type of bomber that would fly subsonically at very low, "under the radar" altitudes within its SLAB (subsonic low-altitude bomber) study. This would lead, via a tortuous route, to the Rockwell B-1B Lancer bomber in the mid-1980s. Some basic research into using the B-70 as a low-altitude penetrator, after first fitting it with terrain-avoidance radar, was conducted in 1960.

President Kennedy endorsed the accountants' verdict on the B-70, but he also considered the program within the context of his wider vision of defense, which embraced the idea of flexible response to a range of limited conflicts that he saw as potentially responsible for "the steady erosion of the Free World." Rejecting Eisenhower's focus on "massive retaliation" clearly had immediate consequences for the B-70, and nuclear weapons systems in general.

McNamara's often-expressed dislike for the cost and complexity of the B-70 program, and his frequent clashes with LeMay as Chief of

NEXT PAGES

SKYBOLT IN COMBAT

This image is of hypothetical B-70A "63-12486" of the 22nd Bombardment Wing (Heavy) "Red Raiders," based at March AFB, California, launching a GAM-87 Skybolt air-to-ground missile during a combat mission against an airfield target behind enemy lines in an imaginary nuclear conflict in about 1965. The "Red Raiders"' 2nd Bombardment Squadron actually converted from the B-47 to the B-52B from March 1963, upgrading to the B-52D in 1966 and then deploying to Vietnam from March AFB. If it had transitioned to the B-70A in 1964–65 instead of the B-52B, the wing would probably have flown Valkyries with a silver finish that reduced the aircraft's infrared signature. Missiles such as the Skybolt that were too large for the weapons bays would have been carried on external pylons. The aircraft has a star-tracker fitted above its nose and small IR scanners and Band 1 antennas on the leading edges and tips of its wings.

Staff from June 30, 1960, led to his refusal to accept it in any role. He inaccurately dismissed its potential and flexibility as a conventional bomber and overemphasized the difficulty of converting it into an air-to-ground missile carrier. Congress was assured that the B-52, with the unproven Skybolt air-launched ballistic missiles, would fulfill this role, but December 1962 would bring the cancelation of Skybolt in favor of submarine-launched ballistic missiles. Achieving approval for his multi-service General Dynamics F-111 program, which was intended to be a US Navy carrier-based interceptor, SAC B-58 replacement, and USAF land-based fighter-bomber, became another excuse for McNamara to withdraw funds from the B-70 and relentlessly pursue its cancelation.

RSB OR NOT RSB

In the face of such implacable opposition, LeMay, NAA, and other USAF generals re-cast the B-70 as a "Reconnaissance-Strike B-70 Weapon System Program," proposing a fleet of 60 RSB-70 aircraft to be in service by 1969, followed by 150 more two years later after research and development work with the first ten. The third XB-70 (AV3) was now to become the XRSB-70, and design work was completed by the end of October 1963. The USAF view, albeit a somewhat rearguard action, was that the B-70 was still a viable bomber. There was also growing support for the XB-70 as a research aircraft for the planned supersonic transport (SST) program.

In fact, the RSB-70 was in most respects similar to the "standard" B-70, but its main role was the carriage of up to 20 900lb air-launched missiles on two rotary launchers that were to be expended in strikes against targets that the ICBMs might have missed. The ability to deliver numerous smaller missiles rather than two or three large nuclear weapons conferred greater mission flexibility. The other main difference was its multi-sensor reconnaissance suite, including a sideways-looking radar installation in the forward fuselage with which it would navigate and locate suitable targets, such as Soviet rail-launched mobile ICBMs.

McNamara acknowledged in January 1962 that "reorientation" of the program in that direction was worth "a great deal more study. Such an aircraft [as the RSB-70] might be useful in providing damage-assessment and reconnaissance information for the re-targeting of the missile force during the attack period. It would also have the capability to attack previously un-located or incompletely destroyed targets." At the time many strategic planners imagined that enough of the USA would survive an apocalyptic nuclear attack to enable such fine calculations still to be made.

Paradoxically, in the same speech, McNamara had stated that "the B-70 is not well suited to an era when both sides have large numbers of ICBMs. It would be more vulnerable on the ground than hardened missiles and it does not lend itself to airborne-alert measures." In simple mathematical terms, an ICBM could hit its target within minutes of a warning rather than the hours that a bomber would take. Essentially, McNamara's January 1962 speech to Congress thoroughly

One disadvantage of the canard was its tendency to increase radar cross-sectional signature, which was already considerable in the case of the XB-70. Canards dated back to the original Wright Brothers' Flyer, and they had been used occasionally to provide a control surface for single-engined designs such as the Focke-Wulf F 19 Ente, Kyushu J7W1 Shinden, and Curtiss-Wright XP-55 Ascender, with varying degrees of success. The idea was revived for the Saab AJ/JA 37 Viggen, variants of the Dassault Mirage and Rafale, and the Eurofighter Typhoon. In these cases its purpose varied between horizontal stabilization, control or lift. For the XB-70's successor, the Rockwell B-1, a small canard was employed to damp down buffeting in low-altitude flight. (North American)

undermined the credibility of the bomber, implying that the RSB-70 was just another attempt to revive the original B-70 program. He judged that the B-70 "would not provide enough of an increase in our offensive capabilities to justify its very high cost. Considering the increased capabilities of ground-to-air missiles, the speed and altitude of the B-70, in itself, would no longer be a very significant advantage. Furthermore, it has not been designed for the use of air-to-ground missiles such as Hound Dog or Skybolt, and in a low-altitude attack it must fly at subsonic speeds."

Two months later, following a presentation by the USAF to the House Armed Services Committee headed by Senator Carl Vinson, a supporter of the B-70, in which Curtis LeMay and the USAF team refuted all McNamara's criticisms of the bomber, the Committee voted 31 to five to restore funding for 60 B-70s, only to be met by McNamara's categorical rejection of the whole RSB-70 concept. McNamara refused to release the funds that Congress had already sanctioned, and he asserted that B-52s and B-58s (which he also planned to withdraw) "could have considerable reconnaissance and bomb damage assessment capability," especially if they arrived "after our missiles have suppressed the enemy's air defenses."

Bleed air was channeled around the YJ93 engines in an attempt to cool the afterburner area and also reduce its infrared signature as a defensive measure. On the ground, the No. 4 engine's exhaust nozzle usually remained open as there was only sufficient internal hydraulic power to close five engines without external power. (Terry Panopalis)

He also argued that an RSB-70 (or "RS-70") would require considerable expenditure for "new high-resolution radar by 1970," and he doubted that existing methods of communication could transmit the reconnaissance data, or that "humans could interpret it fast enough." Finally, McNamara believed that the RSB-70 would require the development of "new air-launched strike missiles" that would have to be "far more accurate than any strategic air-launched missile now in production or development." No doubt McNamara – "Mack the Knife" – had the promising development of Lockheed's SR-71 project in mind as he dismissed the need for a reconnaissance-based Valkyrie. Also, Richard Bissell of the CIA had told Kennedy that Lockheed could turn its new A-12/SR-71 into an intercontinental nuclear bomber, ruling out the need for the B-70 in his view.

Despite the unpromising attitude of the Department of Defense, a team headed by Gen Schriever devoted much time to studying the possibilities of the RSB-70 as a way of saving the B-70 in some form, and they estimated that an example could fly within two years at a development cost of just over $1.5m. Kennedy and Vinson struck a deal in which $50m would be spent on the project out of the $360m Congress originally allocated, thereby appeasing both Vinson and McNamara to some extent.

Further damage to the Valkyrie's prospects occurred in February 1964 when Congress froze the whole program's expenditure at $1.3m. This was sufficient only for two aircraft, and the third, the YB-70A (AV3), which was also referred to as the XB-70B or XRSB-70, was dropped. The final outcome of the hugely expensive B-70 project was, therefore, to be two research aircraft as of March 5, 1964. NAA had lost the two premier defense contracts of the day, the F-108 and the B-70, and its hopes of producing the SM-64 Navaho missile had also been dashed in 1958 when the SM-65 Atlas was selected instead. There were consequences for General Electric too, and engine testing was reduced to a basic flight-test level for the XJ93, without seeking more detailed design improvement and weight reduction. The use of a B-58 Hustler to flight-test the engine was also put on hold.

The publicity surrounding the roll-out of AV1 on May 11, 1964 was part of the unspoken propaganda campaign that was designed to make the world (and the Soviet Union in particular) well aware of the formidable advances made by American aircraft designers. Although President Eisenhower crippled the B-70 project, it was the US Army that suffered the most severe shrinkage during his presidency since he regarded a large army force as a possible source of "military adventurism." Under his successor, John F. Kennedy, the quest for funds to rebuild the army would become one of the new threats to the B-70 program. (North American)

DEFINING THE GODDESS

The first two XB-70s (AV1 and AV2) were to have been built to the same basic specification for use as technology demonstrators, but with minor differences. Neither had operational military equipment. AV2's wing was given five degrees of dihedral to improve lateral stability at medium supersonic speeds, whereas AV1 had the original "flat" wing. The second aircraft had an automatic air intake control system rather than the manual version in AV1 and a 2,800 gallons increase in fuel capacity, as its fifth fuel tank could be effectively sealed, unlike the problematic tank in AV1.

Bigger changes were scheduled for AV3, most notably a doubling of the crew to four to manage the AN/ASQ-28 bombing-navigation systems (including star trackers) and defensive electronics, although the program for the latter had already been canceled. An enlarged weapons bay would have accommodated up to 25,000lb of ordnance. Operational electronics would have included an inertial navigation platform and Doppler radar antennas in the nose and radome. Extra power generation and cooling systems were needed for the considerable amounts of additional electronic equipment.

Later modifications scheduled for AV2 included a trials-only in-flight refueling receptacle ahead of the windshield, an internal missile launcher in the aft weapons bay to test-launch two air-to-ground missiles, and a canard with an extra 20 degrees of sweep-back on its leading edge. The revised canard would also have been fitted to AV3/XRSB-70 prototype and an AN/ARC-90 UHF communications

antenna built into its left vertical stabilizer. A flight control simulator, resembling the one used for the X-15 research aircraft, was ready for use in August 1960

Each one of these aircraft presented extraordinary technical challenges for NAA to overcome, as they did with their X-15 rocket aircraft, among many other projects, but few of those issues appear to have been well understood by McNamara's team, whose main concerns were costs and deadlines. Ground-breaking technical innovation seldom works to those parameters in the way that accountants would like, but Washington's continued skepticism about the B-70's survivability and effectiveness in an increasingly hostile potential combat scenario was even more destructive to the project.

When AV1 was finally rolled out, it was the world's heaviest and most powerful aircraft, the fastest multi-engined bomber and by far the most costly. It also had an extremely prominent radar signature, which would have assisted enemy defenses in targeting it as it sped into hostile airspace. At Mach 3, sudden changes of course to avoid interception were not possible, and the bomber's direction of travel would be easy to plot, giving SA-2 batteries plenty of time to prepare missiles. If such high speed, without "stealth" protection from radar detection, was no longer any guarantee of immunity, the much cheaper alternative of larger numbers of slower, smaller aircraft flying nap-of-the-earth, sub-radar penetrations became more logical.

The "higher and faster" philosophy that had driven military aircraft design up to that point had finally run out of credibility, except perhaps for the SR-71. As the B-70 began to be seen increasingly as a stand-off missile launcher, attention turned to slower types like the B-52, which could carry more missiles over equivalent ranges at much lower cost. Risking such valuable investments as B-70s in an environment where one lucky missile shot could fell a bomber at any altitude seemed increasingly unviable.

The lengthy forward fuselage positioned the XB-70 pilot more than 30ft above the ground on touchdown, with the aircraft at a high angle of attack, limiting his forward vision. This problem was addressed in the Sukhoi T-4 Sotka and Concorde by drooping the entire nose. As the cockpit was more than 110ft ahead of the main landing gear, special techniques for landing and taxiing the aircraft also had to be learned. The extended forward fuselage helped to create a shockwave beneath it that would enter the air intakes, creating air pressure for the engine compressors to use. (North American)

The Valkyrie's massive nose landing-gear unit had the same tires as the main undercarriage wheels. They were painted and impregnated with heat-resistant metallic additives. (AFFTC/Terry Panopalis)

22. Wingtip fold line
23. Gearbox reservoir
24. Hydraulic engine pumps, 4,000psi
25. Weapons bay door (slides to rear, production aircraft)
26. Drag parachute compartment
27. Stellar inertial platform (production aircraft)

28. Doppler radar antenna (production aircraft)
29. Central computer (production aircraft)
30. Flight control runs
31. Fuel lines around fuel tank
32. Hoist point

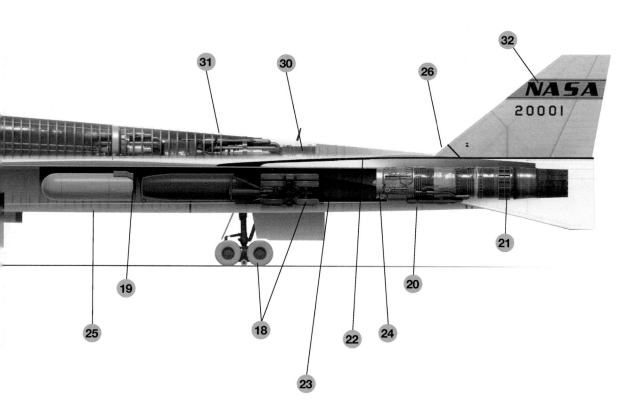

ENCAPSULE, ENCAPSULATE!

Behind the XB-70A's radome was a two-seat cockpit. Probably the most unusual feature of this area was the use of escape capsules for both crew members. The need for better protection for pilots than a conventional ejection seat could offer in high-Mach emergencies had encouraged designers to seek a structure that would enclose the pilot and his seat as he left the cockpit and entered the atmosphere at speeds that could easily tear him apart. NAA initially investigated a system where the entire nose would separate and parachute down, but it soon turned to a capsule system, which was being explored by several manufacturers.

Early experiences with a capsule that completely protected the pilot during a high-speed ejection had not been promising. Mel Apt was killed when the over-elaborate escape capsule in the Bell X-2 proved to be impracticable in a September 1956 accident. NAA ruled out encapsulation for its Mach 6 X-15 research aircraft when it became clear that an appropriate capsule would weigh about 9,000lb.

For its B-58A Hustler, Convair realized that conventional SAC ejection seats provided inadequate protection, so it procured the Stanley Aviation Company Model B encapsulated seat in February 1958. It was pressurized, water-tight, and provided a self-contained environment for the pilot ejecting at any point in the performance envelope. The pilot could close the clamshell doors of the capsule around him while still in the aircraft and he could still fly it in an emergency such as sudden cabin decompression, with limited vision of the instrument panel through a window. Al White demonstrated that this could be done from the XB-70's version of the seat when he encapsulated himself during AV1's 27th flight and controlled the aircraft for ten minutes at Mach 1.4.

Similar Type B capsules for the Valkyrie were derived from the Type A developed by NAA for the F-108, but slightly widened to allow the crew to wear David Clark A/P22S-6 full-pressure suits for flights above 40,000ft. At lower altitudes the crew could work in what the company called a "shirt-sleeve environment." Whereas the Stanley capsule lowered three sections of a clamshell shield over the seated pilot, the NAA version had two molded aluminum honeycomb clamshell doors, one swinging up from below the seat and the other lowered from above it to form an airtight seal. Three small windows allowed sight of the ground, the parachute that deployed above the capsule, and the aircraft instrument panel. If the pilot unlocked his harness inertia reel and put his face against the forward window he could see the entire instrument panel.

The 1,000lb capsule was intended to offer safe ejection at altitudes up to 90,000ft and speeds between 100 and 2,100mph, including low-altitude operations at 200ft and Mach 0.95. Crew could encapsulate and decapsulate manually to cope with a temporary emergency such as sudden cabin depressurization, or ballistically, which involved a one-shot, irreversible automatic process. For the ballistic method,

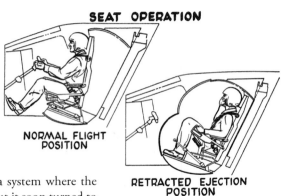

SEAT OPERATION

NORMAL FLIGHT POSITION

RETRACTED EJECTION POSITION

For the Type A capsule in the NAA F-108 the pilot had only to press a "descent button" inside the closed capsule, which pulled back the throttles to idle and set the controls to fly the aircraft into a wings-level descent to 40,000ft, after which it would continue in level flight, as long as there was no major structural problem. The crew could then eject or open the capsules and attempt to resume control. In the XB-70's Type B version, the electrical signaling to the engine control system meant that the "descent button" could still command the engines to throttle back without a mechanical link to the capsule. (NAA)

The Type B capsule for the XB-70, with the seat in the forward (flying) position and the doors stowed. Although the capsule was a complex device, the actual ejection sequence for the crew was similar to that in other contemporary military aircraft, with the notable exception of the upward- and downward-closing clamshell doors that operated once the seat had been drawn back into the capsule. (NAA)

a process taking around two seconds, a pilot first checked that his co-pilot had completed encapsulation. He then raised two hand-grips, retracting the seat into the capsule, automatically stowing the control yoke and exposing two ejection triggers. The clamshell doors closed automatically and the capsule sealed and pressurized itself. He could then remain aboard to try and control the aircraft and reach a lower bailout altitude by using an emergency descent control grip located on the left side of the capsule.

Ejection was initiated by pulling one of the triggers, and the subsequent process was fully automatic. First, the escape hatches in the fuselage above each seat (there were two more for the anticipated extra crew in production aircraft) were jettisoned by a gas-pressurized "hatch remover." A ballistic rocket/catapult then propelled the capsule from the aircraft at a peak thrust of 9,800lb. The capsule's oxygen supply was initiated and gas pressure was released to extend telescopic stabilization booms with small drogue parachutes. A chaff dispensing facility then began to operate and an aneroid device set off the recovery system when the capsule reached an altitude of 15,000ft or less. The main recovery parachute, 34.5ft in diameter, was then deployed and gas was released into an "attenuator" bladder, which inflated below the capsule to soften the landing. Blow-out plugs in the bladder prevented a bouncy landing. The capsule occupant checked the deployment of his main parachute via the capsule's upper window and looked for the attenuator through the lower window.

After a safe landing the parachute could be released by a riser cutter and, for a landing on terra firma, the occupant could then open the doors, step out and use his survival packs. They contained equipment ranging from a whistle to a snare kit for trapping prey. Ejection with the doors open was possible below 15,500ft, and they could be removed by kicking off the lower door if they had jammed in the partially open position. The impact bladder then had to be inflated by pulling a handle in the capsule.

The system was extensively and successfully tested with 52 trial drops at speeds from 25 to 377 knots, including catapult launches from a

B-47's bomb-bay at 41,000ft and others from the under-belly pod of a B-58A at Mach 1.8. Spectacular ground-sled tests took the speed up to 650 knots and flotation tests showed that the capsule would stay afloat on its back. Extra flotation devices would have been included in production examples so that the crew could survive at sea for up to three days. If a crew member inside the floating capsule was injured a ventilation plughole was opened and the capsule could be towed behind a boat to a safer place. Recovery by helicopter, like the various space capsules of later years, was another option for the future.

Al White reported that, "Entering the capsule, particularly when wearing a pressure suit, was difficult due to the lack of space. The pressure seals in the capsule doors were torn loose many times when the pilots entered the capsules." He also noted that some of the emergency controls inside the capsule were hard to see or use when encapsulated, particularly when wearing a pressure suit – a problem which would contribute to a disaster on June 8, 1966.

THE OFFICE

Aboard the aircraft, the XB-70 pilot and co-pilot faced a relatively conventional cockpit arrangement of round dials and several vertical tape displays that had been effective in designs like the F-105 Thunderchief. The cockpit pressure was maintained at an equivalent 8,000ft altitude and temperatures varied between 42 and 105°F. At Mach 3 things became quite noisy, with 96 decibel sound levels recorded in the cockpit, ten decibels above military specification limits. In heavy turbulence the long forward fuselage flexed noticeably, and a 1969 NASA report noted that this "produced unpleasant ride characteristics in the crew compartment under vibrational situations. However, flight control was always maintained, even in heavy turbulence." The cockpit area was extensively instrumented, using an 800-channel digital tape system, to study thermal data, noise levels, acceleration, and vibration.

One of the many test drops of a Type B capsule from C-130, B-47, and B-58 aircraft. The stabilizing booms, with their small drogue parachutes, are extended and the "impact attenuator" bag is inflated below the capsule. (USAF)

OPPOSITE
The pilot's seat in AV1 and the control yoke that was retracted as the seat encapsulated, providing just enough clearance for ejection. (Author's collection)

The XB-70's cockpit was located so high above the ground that the crew required escape ropes and a Sky Genie abseiling device to leave the aircraft for a 17ft descent in a ground emergency, in the very likely absence of sufficiently long ladders. Normally, ground access to virtually any part of the aircraft required complex ladder and platform equipment as seen here, although the aircraft was intended to operate from any B-52-capable base. (USAF)

Ahead of the multi-panel windshield was the second, moveable hydraulic windshield ramp that was raised on hinges and roller assemblies to give a more streamlined 14 degrees windshield slope profile for high-Mach flight rather than the 24 degrees slope of the fixed structure. It had five transparencies of tempered glass and was sealed with a metal bellows arrangement and silicone rubber to prevent air from entering the space between the two screens. Although the aircraft could be flown supersonically with the ramp lowered, this was not recommended for flights above Mach 2.5 as damage to the inner windshield layers and seals could occur. NASA reported that, "With the nose-ramp down the crew has minimum acceptable visibility throughout the flight envelope. The nose-ramp-up position provides aerodynamic fairing to minimize drag and heating at high speeds and virtually eliminates forward visibility." Windshield temperatures of 600°F were later recorded at Mach 3.

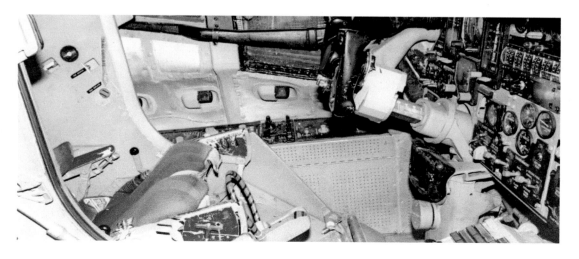

The two weapons bays, located between the intake ducts, would have held up to 20,000lb of standard bombs or nuclear weapons weighing 10,000lb. Air-to-ground missiles with a range of 700 miles were planned, but larger missiles such as the Douglas GAM-87 would have been hung on underwing pylons. The size of nuclear weapons at the time of WS-110A's genesis dictated large weapons bays in a big aircraft. (USAF)

REAR AND LOWER FUSELAGE

Most of the fuselage below the wing consisted of air intakes, with the engine compartment occupying the final 26ft. A 1,200cu ft weapons bay in two 14ft-long sections (including a one-foot unusable area between them) took up part of the space between the intakes. The doors that covered them were not powered on AV1 and AV2 as the bays were not to receive operational equipment. Large, load-bearing access doors for the six engines also had to be incorporated into the lower fuselage.

Strength was therefore the key factor in this relatively hollow section that had to bear the aerodynamic loads on the wings as well as the high external skin temperatures, which would reach 600°F on the leading edges of the flying surfaces and the nose, and the internal temperatures of up to 900°F caused by the engines' heat emissions. The choice of metals giving the necessary strength, lightness, and heat resistance was therefore crucial. Titanium frames, steel beams, and spars were covered with titanium skins on their tops and sides and the engine compartment doors were also fabricated from 6A1-4V(STA) titanium alloy skins to provide strength and resistance to fracturing.

Vertical "tape" instruments show Mach number (left unit) and altitude/vertical velocity (right unit), with the large attitude director indicator between them. The orange "climb schedule" statistics in the center of the control yoke replaced the original NAA logo. Test pilot Alvin White felt that the nose-wheel steering button should have been on the control wheel rather than the "augmentation disengage" switch, which took up the small available space. Without an inertial platform navigation system, the crew's information on attitude and heading was considered "marginally satisfactory." White was also critical of the controls for the Hamilton Air Inlet Control System (AICS) in AV1, and he noted that although the cockpit map case was "of little use to the pilots, it was the only place where extra material could be stored." The pilot had to get out of his seat to access the map case, and he had to keep check lists, pilot's data cards etc., strapped to his legs if they were to be of any use. (Author's collection)

FLYING SURFACES

NAA designers, led by Walt Spivak, placed a canard with a total area of 265.28sq ft on the upper fuselage behind the cockpit. Made of titanium and steel beams, with stainless steel cover plates, the canard was mainly used to trim the aircraft, causing less drag in this capacity than conventional elevators and lending additional lift to the forward part of the airframe at transonic speeds. The whole structure could be deflected between zero and six degrees for trimming, and the trailing edge could be drooped by 20 degrees to form flaps, reducing takeoff and landing speeds. With the flaps lowered, the canard automatically moved to its full nose-down position.

The 105ft span delta wing had six integral fuel tanks. The downward-folding outer wing panels, which would also have contained fuel in production aircraft, were called "tips" by NAA, although they were actually the largest moveable flight control surfaces ever used on an aircraft. Each one covered 500sq ft, roughly the size of a B-58A's wing. The entire wing was swept back at 65.5 degrees and covered 6,297sq ft in area. By comparison, the Avro Vulcan's delta wing covered 3,965sq ft and the B-52H's was 4,000sq ft.

NAA used a multi-spar steel structure with steel panels over an inch-thick honeycomb core, reduced to 0.75in depth for the outer panels. Joining the wings to the center fuselage required more than eight miles of welding for the 80ft long joining surfaces, components, and fuel tanks. For AV2, the introduction of dihedral involved moving the wing outwards slightly, angling it up by five degrees and filling the

gap with honeycomb transition section panels and shear webbing. A disadvantage of the dihedral wing was that, if sideslip occurred in flight, one wing would drop slightly and the sideslip would worsen if the pilot used the elevons to try and raise the wing.

The folding tips, which had a slight kink in their leading edges, had three positions. Below Mach 0.95 or 400 knots they were level with the main wing. Between Mach 0.95 and Mach 1.5 they were in the halfway position and they were fully lowered above Mach 1.6. The halfway and full-down positions of 25 degrees and 65 degrees respectively on AV1 were increased to 30 degrees and 70 degrees for AV2. The tips obviously had to be leveled before landing to prevent impacting the ground at the full-down setting, and a weight-on wheels device stopped them from being lowered on the ground. Furthermore, there were three systems, including an emergency back-up, to ensure that they could be raised when airborne. The crew had a wingtip position indicator on the central instrument panel and a barber's pole indicator to show when the tips were moving to a new setting.

At high speeds their stabilizing effect compensated for the relatively small areas of the vertical stabilizers, and in the full-down position they magnified the shockwave beneath the aircraft, adding five percent extra compression lift. It was calculated that the vertical stabilizers would have needed twice their area of 234sq ft to provide adequate stability at high supersonic speeds without the moveable wingtips.

The tips were electrically controlled by six Curtiss-Wright motorized hydraulic hinges for each side, and the hinge line was covered by a black magnesium-thorium fairing strip. Slight rolling motion could be felt if the tips did not activate completely in unison and a severe control problem would have resulted from markedly asymmetrical operation, requiring both to be raised immediately, a procedure that took over a minute.

AV2 cruises serenely with its wingtips raised. The Valkyrie's unique structure posed restrictions on emergency recovery. Belly landings were ruled out and pilots were told that "under no circumstances should ditching be attempted because the airplane design prevents successful ditching." The briefest glance at the huge intake box is sufficient explanation for that instruction. (Terry Panopalis collection)

The co-pilot had similar vertical tape displays and a control yoke that, in this case, exhibits a fuel tank reference diagram rather than the original "XB-70" logo. The co-pilot of what NAA called "The Great White One" was effectively the flight engineer on AV1, managing the fuel and inlet systems manually among other tasks. Some of the fuel quantity gauges can be seen on the left, and the panel for the AICS, with a white placard, is visible below the control yoke, with further AICS controls on the right side-panel. (Author's collection)

At the trailing edges of each main wing surface were six elevon sections, each with two hydraulic actuators, divided in that way to avoid excessive bending loads. They could move up or down by 30 degrees, providing pitch control when operated symmetrically with fore and aft movements of the control column, and roll control when operated differentially. If the wingtips were lowered the two outer sections of each elevon were locked in the neutral position. After the first few flights test pilot Alvin White found that the outer pair of elevon sections on each wing were providing excess roll power and he neutralized them by lowering the wingtips to the 25 degrees position. Adverse yaw was then reduced as well. Wingtip operation was via a three-position rotary tip position selector switch on the central instrument panel and a two-position, back-up "fold mode" switch.

The vertical stabilizers were unusual in having only about a third of their area as fixed surfaces, while the larger, rudder sections pivoted on hinges placed at a 45-degree angle. They deflected 12 degrees left or right with the landing gear lowered or three degrees with the gear retracted. The rudders were operated by standard foot-pedals, which also operated the wheel brakes and nose-wheel steering. Multi-spar construction and brazed steel honeycomb panels were used to construct the vertical stabilizers. The flying controls had an augmentation control system, operated hydraulically and signaled electrically, which provided automatic damping in all three axes. In test pilot Don Mallick's estimation, the XB-70 "flew well and responded nicely to the pilot's

On the central control panel, the six throttles are the central feature, with controls for the wingtip fold and landing gear above them, TACAN buttons to the right, and the intercom controls to their left. Among the most crucial indicators were the 12 hydraulic pump status lights (upper right). NAA-embossed rudder pedals can be seen to each side of the console. (Author's collection)

control inputs. It handled very well throughout its flight regime with the exception of dampers-off flight around Mach 2.3 to 2.6. In this area the XB-70 had a lateral-directional oscillation that was difficult for the pilot to damp manually."

The 7ft-high rectangular-sectional cavern of each air intake duct channeled air on an 80ft journey to a plenum chamber ahead of three YJ93 engines. Each intake had a variable area bypass system and boundary layer bleed control, with six pairs of interconnected bypass doors, opening upwards and downwards, in the upper surface just ahead of the engines. They could provide up to 2,400sq in of air bypass area. A bleed-air chute was built beneath the forward part of the intake box. Three perforated, moveable panels, or ramps, varied the size of the intake throat to provide air to the engines at the correct speed. They could alter the size of the "throat" from 48 inches to 19 inches depending on airflow requirements.

The XB-70's cavernous left intake duct, looking forward, resembled an urban underpass. (Terry Panopalis collection)

All these devices controlled the shockwaves which slowed the supersonic airflow sufficiently for it to enter the engine compressors at subsonic speed. From its initial entry past the splitter plate at the front end, the air flow was subjected to three stages of controlled shocks as it passed along the duct. The positions of the shocks could be varied, using the variable geometry features, to suit speed and external air conditions. The first shock was generated at the splitter plate to start the ramps operating, and if the shockwave did not enter the inlet tunnel at that stage an "unstart" occurred, causing a drop in engine thrust in that inlet (usually followed by a similar condition in the other one) and unstable aircraft handling. At Mach 2 the intake ramps began to close, restricting the "throat." Reaching Mach 3, the airflow was slowed from 2,000mph to around 600mph for entry to the engine compressors. The inlet system was a very demanding design job, initially taken on by Hamilton Standard but eventually reverting to NAA.

The large intake area contributed to the XB-70's conspicuous radar cross-section (its opponents claimed that this was ten times greater than the B-52's) and there were proposals to install radar-absorbing material on their inner faces to reduce the head-on radar signature to a lower level than the B-52's. The very obvious side-on "spikes" in radar signature caused by the flat fuselage sides would not have helped enemy defenses since the aircraft would have been traveling too fast and high for them to react after noticing the radar trace. NAA also worked on ceramic and metallic coatings to radiate the aircraft's surface heat at wave-lengths that would be hard for Soviet infrared detectors to pick up. These finishes had to be applied in two coats over a polished surface and cured at high temperatures. Production B-70s could have gone into service with a silver-gray version of this finishing process, rather than the gleaming white of the two AVs, although both types of finish presented problems of adhesion to titanium surfaces.

The lower fuselage also accommodated the three massive Cleveland Pneumatic Tool Company steel landing-gear units that weighed a total of 12,000lb. All three used the same 40in wheels and 40 x 17.5in Type VIII B.F. Goodrich nitrogen-inflated tires, impregnated with a silver heat-resistant substance. Two were used on the nose-wheel unit, which could be steered hydraulically through 58 degrees to each side while taxiing, although its inadequate torque meant that considerable engine thrust was needed to turn a slow, heavy Valkyrie. As these wheels were located 65ft behind the pilot's seat, taxi techniques had to be re-learned, particularly when turning, to keep the aircraft within

runway limits. The cockpit's position at the end of the long, flexing forward fuselage also gave the crew a bouncy ride while the nose undercarriage negotiated joins in a concrete runway.

The complex main-gear units each used four-wheel bogie structures that had to fold vertically and rotate through 90 degrees on retraction aft into the fuselage to fit into the restricted well space. As the aircraft approached touch-down the main bogies were held at an eight degrees nose-high angle.

The XB-70's size and weight required massive, complex brake units to stop the aircraft. They were situated between the pairs of main wheels and assembled from 20 revolving discs and 21 fixed discs. Exposed to the air to aid cooling, they still reached temperatures above 2,000°F as they absorbed the massive kinetic energy developed by the aircraft on landing at speeds between 175 and 219 knots. The brakes were never very effective at low taxiing speeds. A small sensing wheel was added in the center of each landing-gear bogie to measure actual ground speed after landing and transmit that data to the brake computers (one for each brake) so that braking pressure was

AV2 approaches the runway with its landing gear correctly positioned and an F-104A-10-LO chase plane in close attendance. During the XB-70A's long-ranging, circular Mach 3 flights, F-104 chase aircraft were positioned at Mountain Home AFB, Idaho, or Hill AFB, Utah, in case the aircraft had to divert to one of those bases. A black radome underside was used for AV2, although its navigation-bombing system was never installed. This aircraft made nine out of the ten XB-70 flights at Mach 3+. Its white paint tended to release heat from the airframe, although the initial paint-job on AV1 also had an unwanted ablative effect when it peeled off under stress. AV2 had 230 instrumented test points rather than the 19 originally installed in AV1. (AFFTC)

GROUND SUPPORT EQUIPMENT FOR XB-70A 62-0207

Typical support equipment for XB-70. Several of each item, particularly fuel trailers, would have been on site.

1. B2 maintenance platform and crew access steps
2. B4 adjustable maintenance platform, extended
3. Type AF/S 32 M1 mobile aerial platform
4. MA-3 air conditioner units
5. Type CT40RS towing tractor
6. MD-3A generator sets
7. Fuel servicing trailer
8. USAF Type 0-11A American LaFrance Airfield Crash Truck
9. North American "school bus" command vehicle
10. Liquid oxygen supply unit
11. Liquid nitrogen supply unit

OPPOSITE
The second XB-70 taxis in along one of Edwards AFB's hardened runways. The brake parachute doors remain open but the 'chutes themselves have been dropped on the runway. On early flights it was common for only two of the three parachutes to deploy. (AFFTC)

limited automatically to prevent skidding. Automatic braking could be selected with a switch in the cockpit or a manual back-up system. Wheel-well doors for all three gear units normally closed when the undercarriage was lowered and locked, a procedure that took around 23 seconds.

The undercarriage was operated by a single handle that was pulled out from the center instrument panel and raised, causing the two utility hydraulic systems to operate the wheel-well doors and initiate the complicated landing-gear extension sequence. Designing and testing the landing gear was a demanding process, with numerous component failures, some of which continued into the flight-test program. The other retarding device during a landing was a trio of 28ft diameter ring-slot braking parachutes, deployed from a compartment above the

SERPENTINE
SIX PACK

Both XB-70s used six single-shaft General Electric YJ93-GE-3 turbojets, each developing 28,800lb thrust at sea level or 19,000lb in military power. Their combined power apparently made the XB-70 the loudest aircraft of its time. Takeoff required all six variable-thrust afterburners, and accelerating half a million pounds of XB-70 took a long runway. Ground-running demanded a clear area of 750ft behind the engine and ear protection was mandatory. Large sound abatement mufflers could be attached to the exhausts with adapter rings for ground tests.

Designed for continuous afterburner operation, the engine pioneered the use of air-cooled titanium turbine blades that allowed higher operating temperatures than conventional steel blades, although resistance to foreign object damage was reduced. The 20ft-long engine was more than 4.3ft wide, and it offered a comparatively favorable 6:1 thrust-to-weight ratio burning JP-6 fuel (designed for the J93), although the afterburner performance tended to be unstable.

A close-up view of AV1's engine compartments, Nos. 1 to 6, and its unique segmented elevons that could move up or down by 30 degrees to provide pitch or roll control. (NASA/Terry Panopalis collection)

Unusually for that time, the engine was ready for the aircraft's first flight after extensive testing for more than 5,000 hours, including 600 hours in Mach 2+ conditions, where it was found that fuel economy for the engine was better than it would have been at slower speeds. The J93 was designed for a maximum altitude of 95,000ft and Mach 3.2, with optimum performance at Mach 3 and 65,000ft. It was ground-tested aboard NB-58A Hustler 55-0662, although the flight-test program for that combination was canceled and the Hustler, as a TB-58A, became the chase aircraft for the XB-70 program instead.

A corrugated alloy sandwich heat-shield, with its inner surfaces gold-plated to reflect the heat, encased ten feet of each engine. NAA used a similar engine-bay shielding process for its A-5 Vigilante. Engine management was by electrical signals from the throttles to the John Oster engine control system for each engine, where a mechanical system took over. There was a wide range of advanced secondary systems. The four hydraulic systems, operating at an unusually high pressure of 4,000psi, used a specially developed lightweight stainless steel and Oronite 70, a new type of fluid. Such high pressure was needed to operate the control surfaces under the extreme aerodynamic forces experienced at Mach 3. The system powered 44 motors and 85 actuators, as well as numerous valves and pumps, all of which were built to tolerate temperatures of up to 630°F.

rear fuselage by a 30in diameter pilot parachute and an 11ft diameter extraction parachute. They could be used as soon as the aircraft landed, at speeds below 220mph.

Although both AVs carried up to seven tons of test instrumentation, they were allowed only very basic avionics, including two UHF radios, an AN/APX-46 IFF transponder, a fairly reliable AN/ARN-65 TACAN radio navigation unit, and an AN/ARN58 instrument landing system. Navigation for test flights was pre-planned, but old-fashioned dead reckoning with assistance from TACAN, chase aircraft, and ground control radars also helped. Autopilots were planned for production B-70s.

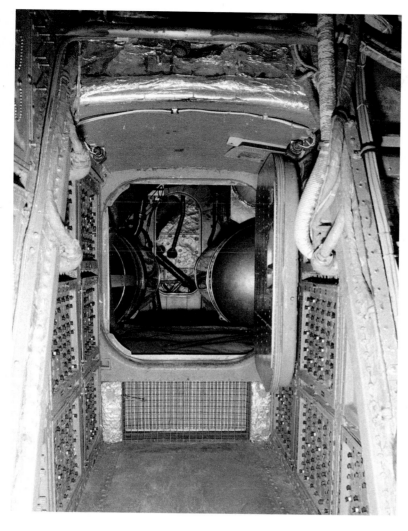

The 12ft-long electronic equipment compartment behind the cockpit, and beyond it the hatchway into the environmental control equipment compartment. (Terry Panopalis collection)

Electronic equipment was housed in a 12ft-long bay behind the cockpit area and a second 21ft-long area beyond that, which was designed to hold the environmental control equipment. Both were pressurized, cooled, and accessible in flight. There was also room for the military systems that would have been ready for production B-70s, including the crucial AN/ASQ-28 bombing-navigation system incorporating a star-tracker and sideways-looking Doppler radar. In its definitive version, the AN/ASQ-28 would have been required to manage and launch weapons at Mach 3. Active and passive defensive avionics with threat warning and evaluation capability, jamming (via a version of the B-52's AN/ALQ-27), and chaff and flare launching were also planned. Some research was conducted into defensive missiles, including one with a warhead that would defuse hostile missiles in flight.

As the flight-test program approached in September 1964 the flight crews were selected and prepared. The initial choice of primary program pilot was Al White. F-100 test pilot Al Blackburn was chosen to back White, but he moved to an office job and was replaced by Zeke Hopkins, who in turn decamped to Edwards AFB and was replaced by Van H. Shepard. White and Shepard went through B-58 Hustler training in 1962. For the USAF, Maj Joe Cotton was assigned as project pilot, with Maj Fitzhugh Fulton, a veteran of many X-plane flights as B-50 and B-52 carrier-plane pilot and project pilot on the B-58, as his deputy.

Knowledge of flight beyond Mach 3 was limited to the first occasion in 1956 when Mel Apt was lost and a series of X-15 flights in 1960 by Joe Walker, leading eventually to a Mach 6.7 flight in 1967. In mid-1963 the fastest jet flight was by the Mach 3 Lockheed A-12, but Al White and his team still had plenty of supersonic territory to explore with the much larger XB-70.

CHAPTER FOUR

THE VALKYRIE'S FIRST RIDE

In the words of the Norse myth describing the Valkyries surrounding Helgi, the holy one,

> *Three times nine girls, but one girl rode ahead*
> *White-skinned under her helmet,*
> *The horses trembling, from their manes*
> *Dew fell into the deep valleys.*

This was one of many occasions on which the airborne warriors protected their king, and it established a powerful image of vengeance from the skies. Richard Wagner's celebration of their sky ride in the 1870 opera *Die Walküre* in *Der Ring des Nibelungen* took eight minutes – rather shorter than the first hop for the XB-70 but no less eventful and dramatic.

Following the roll-out ceremony in May 1964, the flight research program was reduced to 180 hours and AV3, still being assembled, was canceled. NASA had agreed to supply extra instrumentation to add to NAA's suite and collect data that might be of use for the SST. NASA also hoped to continue that research after the USAF had explored the Valkyrie's capability, much as they had done with previous X-planes, but the first stages of testing involved many hours of engine ground-runs and systems checks at NAA's Palmdale facility. Numerous leaks in the hydraulic systems occurred due to vibration in the engine compartments as the six massive turbojets thundered in their box-like bays.

The roll-out of AV2, with its black radome area, on May 29, 1965 was a much less public affair than the debut of the first Valkyrie. Its long, serpentine forward fuselage flexed noticeably in any kind of turbulence, oscillating vertically and horizontally. Al White described the sensation as, "like we were riding on the end of a big fishing pole." (AFFTC)

Servicing vehicles and technicians swarm around AV1 during night-time preparations for its first flight. (NAA/ Terry Panopalis collection)

Taxi trials followed until September 14, revealing a lack of braking power and persistent brake chatter as the linings bedded in, more hydraulic leaks, and a need for great care in turning the aircraft on the ground because of its unusual nose landing-gear position. NASA pilot Don Mallick noted that:

"A big problem when taxiing was guessing the location of the landing gear relative to the taxiway. This made for an interesting sensation during a turn. We had to wait until the cockpit was over the edge of the taxiway, towards the desert before we actually initiated the turn. This ensured that the main gear did not drop off the taxiway on the inside of the turn. It was different from any other aircraft and difficult to get used to. Seated so high above the ground, it was difficult to judge taxi speed. Because we had no ground speed readout in the cockpit we relied on escort vehicles to call out our speed occasionally on the radio. It was hard to stop the aircraft once we had some speed so we didn't want to go too fast. Also, when coming to a complete stop, the pilot had to be smooth in applying the brakes in order not to lock the wheels."

The drag parachutes were tested and the aircraft was taxied to around 120 knots, after which it was thoroughly inspected, with particular attention paid to the hydraulics and the undercarriage. All main-gear tires were replaced, as were several hydraulic valves. White planned to spend 1hr 45min airborne, initially with the landing gear down at 250 knots for the local phase, increasing to supersonic speed at 30,000ft over the Edwards AFB area. In so doing he would earn NAA the traditional bonus (in this case $250,000) for going supersonic on the first flight.

White and Cotton climbed the long crew entry ladder on September 21 and started AV1's engines, although two needed re-starting due to a faulty cut-out switch. "Fitz" Fulton and Van Shepard boarded their TB-58 primary chase aircraft to follow the flight and five T-38 Talons were on hand as chase, camera-ship, and reserve chase aircraft, together with two H-21 helicopters. There was then a two-hour delay while groundcrew replaced a faulty hydraulic pump in the fuel system. The

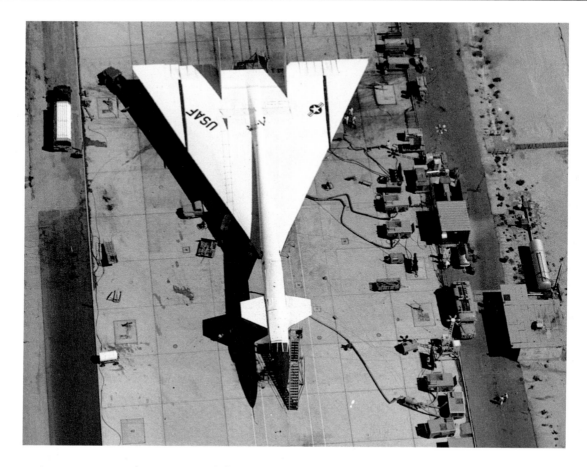

engines were re-started once again and the mighty Valkyrie taxied out (with severe brake chatter still evident – this was never really cured) and accelerated down Palmdale's runway, lighting its afterburners in pairs and lifting off at 205 knots in less than 5,000ft at 0838hrs.

The aircraft climbed steeply away, remaining below the 250 knots landing-gear speed limit and leveling off at 15,000ft. White then tried to raise the canard flap and undercarriage. Although the nose gear retracted properly the two main trucks turned at right-angles to the direction of flight but would go no further due to a valve failure. A chase pilot also reported hydraulic fluid streaks on the lower fuselage. When Cotton lowered the landing-gear handle again the nose gear extended and the main undercarriage members returned to the correct orientation but the main gear doors remained open.

The fault was frustrating because the landing gear had been cycled 20 times on jacks prior to the flight. Realizing that the supersonic prize was out of reach the pilots used their time to explore low-speed handling and stability, noting that there was buffeting around the canard. The number three engine then began to over-speed and had to be shut down. After some more low-speed stability checks White headed for the main runway at Edwards AFB, only 30 miles away, using the chase pilots to give him accurate height indications for a

AV1 on the engine run-up pad at Edwards AFB surrounded by support vehicles. (AFFTC/ Terry Panopalis collection)

OPPOSITE
AV2 streams condensation at Edwards AFB. On takeoff the aircraft usually rotated at 175 knots and the landing gear had to be retracted before it reached 250 knots. Over-rotation would cause an excessively long takeoff run. Pilots of the F-104 chase aircraft occasionally had to fly within 12–15ft of the XB-70's underside to check on the undercarriage. Test pilot George Marrett once had to position a T-38A 15ft below the Valkyrie's jet nozzles so that a cameraman could photograph the jet efflux for studies of the fuel pattern. (NAA/Author's collection)

Groundcrew contemplate the two burned-out rear tires on AV1's left undercarriage truck after the brakes locked on the aircraft's first landing. (AFFTC/Terry Panopalis collection)

smooth touch-down. He used their guidance for his first nine flights before developing a "feel" for the landing situation.

White learned to aim for a touch-down point 2,500ft from the runway threshold to compensate for the cockpit's height above the runway and distance from the main landing gear. Landing at an angle of attack (AOA) greater than 11 degrees would make the jet nozzles scrape the runway. The windshield nose ramp, also angled at 11 degrees, duly acted as a visual guide for the correct attitude. When it appeared to be horizontal to the horizon the aircraft was at an 11-degree AOA.

On that first touch-down the landing gear misbehaved. The left unit remained in the flat, "ground" position rather than pivoting so that the rear wheels would make contact first. On the two rear wheels the brakes were locked, causing the tires to blow out and starting a small fire in the unit as the aircraft made its 10,800ft landing run pursued by three fire tenders. Repairs, using new parts and some from the canceled AV3, took eight hours before the XB-70 could be moved, including the replacement of several brakes and two engines after the No. 2 engine was found to have ingested debris on landing. Despite the problems, Al White declared himself "very delighted with the way things went today."

Modifications and checks were completed by October 5, when there was still a chance of a $125,000 bonus for supersonic speed on the second flight. The pilots planned to test for flutter at various speeds before hitting Mach 1.1 at 35,000ft. Two full cycles of undercarriage retraction were made soon after takeoff and the flight seemed fine until

ALVIN SWAUGER WHITE

Al White was born in California in 1918. He enlisted in the US Army Air Corps in 1941 and was posted to the 355th Fighter Group, the "Steeple Morden Strafers," in England flying P-51D Mustangs. After taking a degree in mechanical engineering postwar he joined the USAF's Flight Training Center, working on fire-control systems for the F-86D Sabre and F-89D Scorpion. White graduated from the USAF's Test Pilot School at Edwards AFB in 1952 and joined NAA in May 1954, where he tested the F-86 Sabre, F-100 Super Sabre, and F-107. As chief test pilot he made the first flights of the F-100C and F-100F Super Sabre. He was Scott Crossfield's back-up pilot for NAA's share of the X-15 program, for which he completed all the training and preparation and made many chase flights but, unlike Joe Walker, never flew the black rocket plane. In 1957 White was selected as project pilot for the XB-70. He made 49 Valkyrie flights as pilot and 18 as co-pilot.

During his combat career he was awarded a DFC and ten Air Medals, and his test flying earned him the Octave Chanute Award, Harmon International Trophy, Iven C. Kincheloe Award,

Alvin White (right), with Lt Col Joe Cotton in a pressure suit, trying out the Valkyrie's capsule seat. (AFFTC/Terry Panopalis collection)

and the American Academy of Achievement Golden Plate Award, among others. He joined the airline TWA in 1966, working on research and development, and died in April 2006.

a utility hydraulic warning light began to glow at 28,000ft, raising the specter of total hydraulic loss. Later inspection showed that a hydraulic line had come adrift inside the No. 1 fuel tank, leaking its fluid into the tank and creating an awkward repair situation later.

In this emergency the instructions were to lower the undercarriage while there was still some hydraulic pressure in case the No. 2 hydraulic system also failed. Al White had to resort to the emergency gear extension lever to get the undercarriage down safely, as the main systems were unable to do so. With some uncertainty about the brakes, he landed the aircraft on a dry lake area with only two brake parachutes operative and rolled for 10,000ft. It was obvious that the aircraft had shed some of its pristine white finish where the wings, forward fuselage, and canard had flexed slightly during the flight. The hydraulic problem was eventually remedied several flights later by fitting flexible 4,000 psi hydraulic lines in the No. 1 fuel tank area.

AV1 was ready for its third hop on October 12 – a faultless flight in which a speed of Mach 1.1 was reached for 15 minutes at 35,400ft. Directional control and stability were explored both with and without the stability augmentation system. This time a considerable area of paint finish was lost and the Valkyrie returned to base looking as if it had passed through a belt sander. A complete re-finish was in order, but flight 4, on October 19, proceeded with a still-scruffy airframe until the No. 3 engine had a severe stall during the takeoff run and Al White had to abort the flight to allow checks. This involved de-fueling the aircraft, but during that process a fuel truck caught fire and exploded, killing a NAA technician and injuring four others. The XB-70 was unscathed, however, and the flight was re-scheduled for October 24.

Flight 4 was an opportunity to test the wingtips at their 25 degrees down position and to establish a new record for sustained supersonic flight with a run of 40 minutes and a maximum speed of Mach 1.42 at 46,300ft. With its basic airworthiness proven AV1 was returned to Palmdale, where it had to be used for four months of extensive non-destructive, proof-load structural testing in the absence of funding for an airframe dedicated to that purpose. It was also a chance to strip what remained of the 1,000lb of thick white finish and repaint the aircraft with a thinner coat, including the areas beneath the rear fuselage that had previously been left in bare titanium. Many parts of the structure such as wing boxes, escape hatches, and sections of the fuselage were chosen for replicating purely as test specimens. A few, such as the control surface structural boxes, were cloned and tested to the point of failure.

SUSTAINED SUPERSONICS

Flight testing resumed on February 16, 1965 with a 70-minute sortie, including 40 minutes at Mach 1.6 and 45,000ft. The wingtips were lowered to the full 65 degrees position for the first time and Lt Col Cotton's reaction was that the aircraft "was born to fly with the tips down." This successful flight was marred only by partial failure of the drag parachutes for the third time. Lt Col Fulton was co-pilot for the sixth flight nine days later, although it was curtailed by a further outbreak of hydraulic leaks. After yet more modification of the hydraulic systems the seventh flight was made on March 4, with an hour of continuous supersonic cruise to Mach 1.85 and 50,200ft.

With the eighth flight three weeks later, the first with Van "Shep" Shepard as co-pilot, the Valkyrie passed Mach 2 and sustained it for 40 minutes, adding another 34 minutes above Mach 1 to establish a record for the longest supersonic flight to date. It reached 56,100ft in a long circuit from Edwards AFB down to Salt Lake City and back, trailing sonic booms most of the way and amassing a vast bank of data from the on-board test equipment. It also inadvertently "boomed" Las Vegas twice in the early morning, causing numerous complaints. These supersonic flights usually took place in a corridor 600 miles long and 170 miles wide and lasted for up to 2hrs 27min. Booms would be measured at five monitoring sites on 51 of the XB-70s' 129 flights throughout their five-year test program.

Flight 9 was less successful due initially to yet another spate of hydraulic leaks that obliged White to return to Edwards and land on the concrete runway, as the hard desert surface was experiencing its brief, annual flooding that leveled out the compacted sand each winter. Touching down at 210 knots and 419,000lb (the heaviest landing ever recorded at Edwards), he just managed to stop within the runway's length by using the drag parachutes. The tires had absorbed so much heat in the prolonged, heavy braking needed to stop the aircraft that

Looking every bit the sinister serpent, AV1 taxis out for its fifth flight on February 16, 1965 with White and Cotton in the cockpit. On this flight the wingtips were folded at 65 degrees for the first time. (AFFTC/Terry Panopalis collection)

The Nos. 4, 5, and 6 engines (numbered from the right) that all sustained major damage to their guide vanes and compressor blades after part of the apex of the intake leading edge broke away during the 12th flight by AV1. There were also gashes on the duct floor and the fairing between the Nos. 4 and 5 engines. (AFFTC)

one of them exploded 45 minutes after the landing. On the 11th flight, AV1 was briefly out of control at 64,000ft and Mach 2.2 when failure of another hydraulic valve and a solenoid prevented data from reaching the flight augmentation system, causing the nose to rise uncontrollably. Fortunately, the valve reopened in time for White to stabilize the aircraft.

Far worse was to come on flight 12, the first to be made at more than 500,000lb weight. White and Fulton took the aircraft to 65,000ft, reaching Mach 2.6 with the wingtips down and the windshield up, just over an hour into the flight in which they were testing stability and remaining above Mach 2 for 50 minutes. At that speed there was noticeable vibration in the air intake for the three starboard engines, and the intake stalled briefly. Fulton operated the bypass doors to try and clear the "unstart" condition by re-positioning the shockwave. After several attempts to stabilize the engines, in and out of afterburner, he shut down the three offending YJ93s but severe yawing oscillations continued, together with a strong buzzing vibration in the right air duct (caused by the initial shockwave rapidly passing in and out of the intake opening) that could have led to structural failure unless it was suppressed.

White reduced power on the three good engines by changing the exhaust nozzles' positions, but an automatic lock-up system then operated and reduced the engines' power to idle, suggesting to the pilots that all these engines had failed as well. White dived the aircraft to windmill the engines, providing basic electrical power, and attempted to air-start the No. 3 engine on the left side, which was in fact already running at idle thrust. This process initially stopped the engine, which was the only one providing electrical power via a generator at that time. After a few seconds without any power an emergency generator automatically restored electricity. White realized the problem with the three left engines and brought them all back to full power. He also tried to restart the No. 5 engine on the right side, but it would only develop 85 percent thrust. However, it did power an emergency generator.

As the aircraft descended to 20,000ft the chase pilots caught up and relayed the bad news that part of the V-shaped splitter at the front of the intake structure had broken away. White continued on towards Edwards and lowered the undercarriage, only to find that the flaps would not come down. He therefore had to touch down at 210 knots and roll for around 13,000ft of the dry lake-bed as the drag parachutes did not extend and the nose-wheel steering was also faulty.

MACH 3 MILESTONE

On AV1's 17th flight (October 14, 1965) White and Cotton climbed to 32,000ft and the speed was pushed to Mach 1.7 at 39,000ft. Like other X-plane pilots, White found that his instruments had difficulty in keeping up with the aircraft's rapid acceleration into a circuit that took it over parts of seven states and reached Mach 3 near Rock Springs, Wyoming.

The work-load was heavy, as usual for the XB-70. Fuel management was complex and intake duct positions had to be monitored and usually operated manually by the co-pilot to avoid violent "unstarts." At Mach 2.6 and 67,000ft the white warrior skirted Salt Lake City and accelerated to Mach 2.9 and then through Mach 3 at 70,000ft for the first and last time for this XB-70. No aircraft of its size and weight had reached anything close to that speed previously. The performance was even more impressive when it was found that an XB-70 could reach Mach 3 within 15 minutes of takeoff, accelerating to Mach 1.5 and, at 50,000ft, pressing on to Mach 3. All this had been achieved within 25 hours total flight time and a year from the first flight without any aerodynamic changes to the design.

At 70,000ft on October 14, the Valkyrie was still accelerating but White, who had noticed some flutter at Mach 3, had to make a series of trim changes which reduced their altitude. Climbing again towards 70,000ft and hitting Mach 3.04, the crew heard a loud bang after two minutes. White slowed down and began a descent. At 34,000ft he began a series of other test goals for that flight, but a message from one of the chase jets informed him that a substantial area of skin on the inner leading edge of the left wing was missing. The crew returned to Edwards immediately, but AV1 was limited to Mach 2.6 for the rest of its test career. It was hoped that any structural problems with the honeycomb skins would be solved with the second XB-70.

As White shut down the engines it was obvious that a triangular section of honeycomb structure at the tip of the intake splitter had broken away and passed into the intakes. Only one of the six engines escaped damage by it and the rest had to be rebuilt by General Electric. It was the first occasion on which a large section of steel honeycomb had broken from the airframe at high speed, but not the last. During the July 1965 phase of testing, when speed was pushed up to Mach 2.8 at 68,000ft, sections of honeycomb structure were stripped off parts of the fuselage and above the wing, but without further consequences.

The pace of the flight program picked up in the final weeks of 1965, peaking at one each day at the end of November, but by then the second Valkyrie had entered the game. Rolled out on May 29, 1965 and incorporated into the testing from July 17, AV2 (62-0207) had many improvements in addition to the increased stability resulting from the five degrees of wing dihedral. On its early flights White noticed the effect of the dihedral at lower speeds. The hydraulic systems that had been a constant headache throughout AV1's testing were more robustly constructed, supported, and brazed, with additional lengths of flexible hose like the ones installed in AV1's No. 1 fuel tank area. It had a fully functioning No. 5 fuel tank in the rear fuselage, unlike AV1. The work-load involved in managing the air inlet system was alleviated by an automatic air induction control system, with a standby manual back-up, although it did occasionally tend to recycle itself at high speed, initiating unstarts.

AV2 easily went supersonic on its maiden flight, reaching Mach 1.51 at 42,000ft en route to Edwards AFB. After seven years as chief test pilot, Al White handed control of AV2 to Joe Cotton for its second flight and he transferred to the rear seat of the TB-58A for AV1's 21st flight on November 18 so that Cotton and Van Shepard could fly the Valkyrie on a performance and airspeed calibration mission. AV2

A chase pilot's view of AV1 about to touch down at the end of a successful flight. An Air Force Flight Test Center H-21C Shawnee rescue helicopter follows the landing as a precaution. The Valkyrie's pilot sat 110ft ahead of the main landing gear, complicating the development of a "feel" for accurate touchdown from his position about 40ft above the runway as the wheels made initial contact with the ground. Al White found that parking the aircraft precisely was hampered by poor visibility and the unpredictable behavior of the nose-wheel steering, which varied in its rate depending on the load on the nose landing gear. The extended, unsupported "neck" structure was also subjected to fatigue-inducing flexing motions when taxiing. (USAF)

crept up toward Mach 2, with careful monitoring of its honeycomb skin, and soon achieved a 40-minute dash above Mach 2.5. On the 16th flight, with White back in the left seat, AV2 hit Mach 2.9, but an oil pump failure wrecked the No. 4 engine and the No. 6 engine overheated. Mach 3.05 was finally achieved in a two-minute burst on January 3, 1966. There was no damage to the structure, so the aircraft made a sustained 15-minute Mach 3 flight at 73,000ft on February 17.

Flight tests progressed smoothly until March 7, 1966 when AV1 chose to revisit its previous hydraulic and landing gear eccentricities. Both main hydraulic systems lost pressure during the flight, forcing Shepard and Cotton to return to base and attempt to lower the undercarriage while they could. The nose gear came down but the left main unit had

The famous "tip-toe" landing of March 7, 1966, in which XB-70 AV1 veered far off the runway during its three-mile run with the two gear units in totally different positions. Undercarriage problems on several occasions during the test program prompted the visual inspection of the gear by a chase pilot prior to all landings. (AFFTC/Terry Panopalis collection)

rotated into the correct landing direction before fully extending itself, leaving the front wheels angled nearer to the ground than the rear pair. Worse, the chase pilot reported that the left unit had rotated correctly but its wheel truck was at a near-vertical position. After circling for as long as they could, trying all the back-up alternatives without success, the pilots were advised to attempt a landing on the lake-bed, hoping that ground contact would level the wheels.

Shepard touched down and the XB-70 immediately veered off to the right, so he used the No. 6 (extreme right) engine to try and correct this, although the extra thrust increased their speed. Luckily, the vast area of the dry lake allowed AV1 to complete a three-mile landing run, but with a curve of over 100 degrees and the right landing gear still running on two wheels.

The first Valkyrie was not alone in having a tricky undercarriage. AV2's nose gear gave White and Cotton an unpleasant surprise during their April 30, 1966 flight when it collided with its main door while retracting after takeoff. Two touch-and-go landings, use of the emergency system, and a few high-g maneuvers failed to free the unit from the battered door. Landing with it in that position would almost certainly have written off the aircraft and its crew. After the technicians had pondered the problem, NAA's undercarriage specialist, Bob McDonald, decided that a short-circuit had tripped some circuit breakers and he suggested that a paperclip could be used to bypass the sequencing switch and restore hydraulic power to the landing gear. Cotton could not find a paperclip but he ingeniously fashioned a wire connector from a part on his oxygen hose. He found a screwdriver and a flashlight and located the offending circuit beneath a terminal board. The trick worked and the gear came down, but their troubles were not over.

When White touched down, hoping to lower the nose gently onto the wounded nose-wheel tire, it was immediately clear that the main gear brakes were locked. Six tires burst and fire broke out, seriously

AV1 is seen from the air on March 7, 1966 at the end of its three-mile landing on a "tip-toe" undercarriage, half a mile off course and at a final angle of 110 degrees to the intended direction. (AFFTC/Terry Panopalis collection)

AV2 also experienced undercarriage difficulties. On its 37th flight (April 30, 1966) a sequencing error pulled the gear up before the door had fully opened so that the edge of the door was jammed between the two wheels, cutting into the left tire as the sharp outer skin of the door peeled away. The chase TB-58A Hustler monitored the so-called "paperclip flight" from close quarters. (AFFTC/Terry Panopalis collection)

damaging the undercarriage units. Then the nose wheel thudded down and the resulting vibration snapped the instrument boom off the aircraft's nose. But AV2 had been saved, and fortunately there were spare undercarriage bogies available from the canceled AV3 and a repaired unit from AV1. Two weeks later it was airborne again.

The May 19 flight by White and Cotton fulfilled one of the original contract conditions which was to prove that the XB-70 could travel at Mach 3 for at least 30 minutes. Their flight that day covered 2,400 miles at an average speed of 1,500mph, with 32 minutes at Mach 3.06. The structure was able to cope with temperatures of 620°F and there seemed no reason why Mach 3 could not be sustained for up to 2.5 hours on full fuel tanks. The 1957 parameters set out in WS-110A were at last being realized, albeit too late for the B-70 as a bomber.

VALKYRIE DOWN

When the XB-70s completed their Phase 1 (manufacturer's) stage of the test program in June 1966 they had already participated in the National Sonic Boom Program (NSBP). A range of supersonic aircraft laid booms over the Edwards area where NASA and USAF ground sensors recorded and analyzed the effects. Phase 2, also a USAF/NASA

NEXT PAGES
THE TIP-TOE LANDING

XB-70 62-0001 makes its famous "tip-toe" landing on March 7, 1966. A minor hydraulic failure required pilot Van Shepard to try to lower the undercarriage before hydraulic pressure fell below the point where this was possible. The right undercarriage unit did not fully lower and its rear pair of wheels was slightly higher than the front set, rather than lower as it should have been. The left unit jammed with the four-wheel bogie in a near vertical position and slightly twisted inwards. After touch-down the aircraft swung round in a three-mile, 110 degrees curve, with its left wing lower than the right one. Damage was limited to the undercarriage operating system and the aircraft was flying again two weeks later.

initiative, was more specifically targeted at SST research, for which a Mach 3 aircraft's input was particularly relevant. Additional NASA instrumentation was installed in AV2.

White and Cotton managed to lower the nose gear for the April 30, 1966 "paperclip" landing, but the brakes locked and six main tires blew out. Crash crews quickly extinguished the resulting fires. (AFFTC/Terry Panopalis collection)

With NASA's increased input came a new NASA pilot, Joe Walker, fresh from the X-15 program. For the USAF, Maj Carl Cross (aged 40, with recent Vietnam experience) was enrolled and they began to replace the original Valkyrie flyers, Al White and Joe Cotton. Both men put in training time on the TB-58A and many hours in the simulator to prepare them for XB-70 flights in June. Tragically, Maj Cross's familiarization flight in AV2 was to be his last.

Their June 8 flight (call-sign 207) was to be the first of two for AV2 that day, and the objectives included airspeed calibration and the second NSBP sonic boom run. It was an undemanding mission but ideal as an introduction for Cross. Al White took off at 0715hrs and completed the set tasks by 0830hrs. There was then an additional photo-shoot run, requested by General Electric to publicize five aircraft powered by its engines. Clay Lacy's General Electric-powered Learjet photo aircraft was on hand for a formation led by AV2, flanked on the left by Cdr Jerome Skyrud and E. J. Black in a NAS Point Mugu-based US Navy F-4B Phantom II and a T-38A Talon flown by Capt Peter Hoag, with Joe Cotton in the rear seat. Off the Valkyrie's right wing was a NASA F-104N Starfighter with Joe Walker aboard and a YF-5A piloted by John Fritz.

The group maintained a racetrack pattern at 25,000ft through some cumulus cloud for 30 minutes at 300mph. It was a chance for Maj Cross to fly one lap to experience the XB-70's controls. The formation had to close in several times to suit the cameramen and hold position for another 15 minutes when a USAF F-104D photo aircraft also joined in. On the final circuit, three minutes before the Learjet was due to leave, the crews were informed of a B-58A approaching at higher altitude and all the pilots except Walker reported that they had spotted it. Possibly Walker was looking for it while his F-104N (N813NA) inexplicably moved slightly closer to the Valkyrie and then rose suddenly so that the left tip of its horizontal stabilizer touched the XB-70's drooped wingtip.

The fatal formation, with AV2 flanked on the left by Peter Hoag and Joe Cotton in a T-38A and a Naval Missile Center F-4B flown by Cdr Jerome Skyrud and E. J. Black. General Electric's chief test pilot John Fritz is flying an F-5A on the extreme right, next to Joe Walker's NASA F-104N. Moments later this orderly progression turned to chaos and disaster. (AFFTC)

The Starfighter was probably further destabilized as it entered the XB-70's wingtip vortex. Inverted, it passed across the XB-70's rear fuselage, taking off the right vertical stabilizer and the majority of the left one, before bursting into flames with the loss of one of the world's most skilful and experienced test pilots. The fighter was cut in half behind the cockpit by the Valkyrie's vertical stabilizer and the forward section then smashed into the left wing, causing severe damage to the upper surface. In a few seconds White worked out that the calls of "mid-air, mid-air!" that he was hearing actually applied to the far-away rear end of his own aircraft since no-one had told him directly what had happened. Cotton in the T-38A, referred to "two verticals . . . came off, left and right" and White knew theirs was the only twin-tailed aircraft in the pack.

The stricken Valkyrie continued to fly normally for 16 seconds and then began a slight rolling motion. White tried to correct it, but without vertical stabilizers this increased the instability and the huge aircraft started a snap roll to the right and then entered an uncontrollable, inverted right-hand spiral descent, spilling fuel from its damaged wing. Cotton saw a large section of the left wing break away as AV2 entered a flat spin.

White encapsulated, but his right arm got trapped between the upper capsule door and the bailout handle as the doors closed. To eject at that point would have cut off his projecting elbow on the hatch frame above his head. With the doors partly open his intercom was inoperative so that he could not help Cross or talk to him, although he could "see his helmet, bobbing around. There was nothing I could do to help Carl." Possibly he was injured and rendered unconscious during the initial,

unexpected snap roll. Cross's seat was not retracted into his capsule. Ballistic (automatic) encapsulation was triggered but the forward forces acting on the spinning Valkyrie were too great for the seat retractor to pull the seat back and begin the ejection system. It had blown its relief valve due to the excessive load.

Al White managed to release his arm after an agonizing 80 seconds of effort and he ejected with the capsule doors still partly open. The parachute deployed immediately, tipping him forward in his seat, and he watched the tumbling wreckage of his aircraft pass close beneath him as it fell at about the same rate. He closed the capsule door fully to shut out his vertiginous situation and tried to inflate his attenuator bag beneath the capsule. It had not deployed because the doors were partly open on ejection, covering the bag, and White could not locate the manual back-up lever.

About two minutes after the original collision the XB-70 hit the ground near Barstow, California, with an impact that White could clearly hear. His capsule drifted away from the blazing pyre and it hit the ground with a considerable impact moments later so that his seat was partially torn from its mountings by the 44g force. His heels made indentations in the capsule floor. White extricated himself through an 18in gap in the capsule doors despite arm and back injuries, wrapped himself in his parachute to alleviate the coldness of his shocked state, and awaited rescue.

Don Mallick, who would later fly the XB-70 himself, had just returned from a weather check flight in F-104N NASA 812 when he noticed two columns of black smoke east of Edwards. When he was told the bad news he and flight surgeon Dr Jim Roman took off in a Bell 47G helicopter to investigate. As they reached the crash site they saw, "The once proud ship was lying on the ground as if it 'pancaked' in a spin. It was flattened into the desert, its formerly white

Walker's F-104N, sliced in two behind the cockpit when it struck AV2's right vertical stabilizer, bursts into flames as it tumbles away behind the mortally damaged XB-70. The latter flew normally for a further 16 seconds before it snap-rolled to the right and then entered an uncontrollable, inverted right-hand spiral descent, spilling fuel from its damaged wing. About two minutes after the original collision the XB-70 hit the ground near Barstow, California. (USAF)

surface charred gray and black. The majority of the fuel had burned off and the big black smoke columns were gone, replaced by thin streamers of white smoke. The stainless steel airframe was flattened and shattered. The six round engine nozzles were now oval-shaped, but it was surprising how much of the structure had survived the fire." Test pilot George Marrett, circling the site in a radio-relay T-38A, saw that some parts were still burning intensely.

Mallick discovered that the remains of Carl Cross were still inside the wreck, but Al White was alive with severe injuries. Mallick and Dr Roman set off in search of the crashed F-104N and soon found another flattened, smoking wreck 22 miles away. "The center of it glowed white hot like burning magnesium." Some distance away they discovered the nose section with Joe Walker's body still strapped into his seat, and it was clear that he had been killed during the original mid-air collision. Leaving the rest of the recovery to a USAF team, they used their helicopter to chase off an illegally snooping Press helicopter and returned to Edwards, astonished that such a disaster could have befallen the Valkyrie and its escort.

Maj Cross's capsule was too badly damaged to yield any definite conclusions regarding its lack of success, although it showed that he had pulled one of the ejection handles. The lack of an operable "hot mike" between the capsules prevented the investigators from finding out what he might have said to White, or any advice he might have otherwise received from the pilot, while trying to encapsulate. Possibly a conventional ejection seat would have worked better in the circumstances.

Mallick returned to the site several times to collect debris for the official inquiry board as its members pored over the many photographic images of the collision. Among the fragments they found was the crucial section of the F-104N's tailplane. Examination revealed the imprint of the formation light on the XB-70's wingtip. Calculations showed that within eight feet of the wingtip the power of the swirling air vortex it created would equal the effect of maximum roll control in the small-winged F-104N, making a collision inevitable. The reason for Walker's hazardous proximity to the wingtip remained elusive and theories abounded, even in the official inquiry, including several that he was distracted by other aircraft near the formation or that he did not notice his fighter's slight drift towards the Valkyrie. Possibly he was focusing on the Valkyrie's fuselage to maintain formation and could not see the wingtip. The disaster became one in aviation history's long catalog of unsolved mysteries.

There were inevitable recriminations about the wisdom of allowing such a close-formation publicity session, requested by John Fritz and approved by Joe Cotton and their immediate superiors, although permission from higher authority was not sought. Col Albert Cate, Cotton's boss, was blamed and sacked and two other officers were reprimanded. The loss of AV2 and the pilots was clearly a terrible blow to the program. Apart from the financial loss (more than $230m for the two aircraft alone), the full burden of continued research had to be borne by AV1 until its final flight in February 1969.

CHAPTER FIVE

NASA AND BEYOND

To take the research program forward, much of the instrumentation that AV2 had been carrying had to be replicated in AV1 so that it could assume the former's place in the sonic boom program within Phase 2. In all, 250 sonic booms were to be analyzed to assess the likely environmental impact of a Mach 2.7 airliner. Its undercarriage repairs and other modifications were carried out and, incredibly, some of the recording equipment and a set of eight improved wing-fold hinges were rescued from the wreckage of AV2 and installed in the first Valkyrie. Modifications were recommended for the capsule, including dual seat retractors and a reduction in the survival pack to reduce weight. Effective skin repairs were devised to cure the previous skin-peeling problem and a bob weight mechanism for the rudders was installed to ensure directional stability during an intake unstart.

New crew members also had to be found. Although Alvin White had returned to flight status only three months after the June 8 crash, he left the XB-70 program and joined TWA. "Fitz" Fulton left the USAF to avoid being posted to a staff assignment and joined NASA to become its primary XB-70 pilot. Don Mallick trained on the TB-58A and B-52 to replace Joe Walker, on Chuck Yeager's recommendation, as project pilot for the NSBP sonic boom flights. Joe Cotton and Ted Sturmthal made the USAF-crewed flights. The two crews also manned the TB-58A chase aircraft and alternated with each other as senior pilots on the XB-70.

NSBP was equally funded by NASA and the USAF in Phase 2 of XB-70 testing, with NASA directing its technical aspects. The Valkyrie was the only available aircraft to provide realistic simulation of the

Black smoke pours from six J93 engines as they are wound up for one of NASA's December 1967 noise tests. Numerous microphones were positioned behind the aircraft. (NAA/Terry Panopalis collection)

Lt Col Joe Cotton (left), the USAF project pilot for the XB-70, with his backup pilot, Maj Fitzhugh "Fitz" Fulton, who later became NASA's chief test pilot. (AFFTC/Terry Panopalis collection)

The Valkyrie's most predatory pose was when it flew with the wingtips lowered, cruising at high-altitude. The wingtips were so-called probably because they originally took 20 percent of each wing, but were later increased in area to 40 percent. Al White commented that the tips "introduced some new characteristics in the airplane that had not been experienced before, such as wide variation in directional stability, roll power and dihedral effect." Downwards-pointing tips had been designed into aircraft like the NAA F-108 and BAC TSR2 to combat Dutch roll, but they were at a fixed angle. (NASA)

projected SST, and it could fly at altitudes above 70,000ft, carrying the required instrumentation. NASA had suggested its use for this research in May 1962, and SST development was authorized in June 1963. Although AV1 was still limited to Mach 2.5, its modifications allowed a speed increase to Mach 2.6, closer to the conjectured SST target, although it never exceeded Mach 2.55 during Phase 2.

AV1 completed its NSBP flights on January 17, 1967 and the analysis of the sonic booms added to the growing doubts about the feasibility of the supersonic transport proposals amidst extended political wrangling in respect to the costs and desirability of the project. Debate and research continued until Congress voted to end all SST funding on May 20, 1971. AV1 had completed a total of 160hrs 18min flight time.

NAA offered its own SST proposal as early as July 1961 based on the construction of two additional XB-70As as SST development vehicles. They would have tested the SST's proposed Lightweight Gas Generator engine (replacing two J93s). Military equipment behind the cockpit would have been replaced by sample passenger cabins, containing from 36 to 76 four-abreast seats in the 8ft 4in-wide "swan-neck" forward fuselage. Some of the internal fuel would have been re-housed in the weapons bay, giving a range of up to 4,000 miles depending on the size of the seating area. At Mach 3 the flights would have been short enough to eliminate a galley. Although the "Valkyrie liner" was only a feasibility demonstrator, NAA believed it would have given the USA a head-start in the SST field up to five years before a purpose-built SST could have been flown. The company also produced an outline of a 450,000lb, Mach 2 SST for up to 150 passengers, or military cargo and troops for the USAF.

The basic B-70, however modified for passenger use, could never have been an SST. As "Fitz" Fulton pointed out, "The normal light gross weight approach speed of approximately 200 knots is much too high for an SST and causes some apprehension when maneuvering from an offset approach to line up with the runway." He also noted

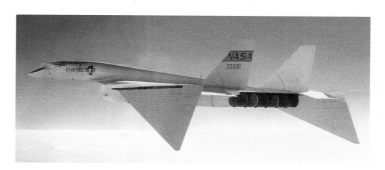

that the complex XB-70 AV1 landing gear had failed in some way on seven of its 78 flights, and observed that, "The XB-70 cannot be landed without probable catastrophic failure if the nose-gear fails to extend. Therefore, bailout would be required. Obviously bailout is not the solution to a serious SST landing-gear malfunction." He advocated an SST undercarriage that was "relatively simple in design and operation."

Various potential life extension projects were promoted. In 1966 a faster carrier aircraft was sought in order to give the X-15 rocket plane a Mach 3 start at very high altitude. Its usual NB-52 mother-ship required the X-15 to accelerate from subsonic speed when dropped at around 45,000ft, limiting its potential Mach 6+ performance with a rocket motor that burned for a few minutes only. A "slingshot" Mach 3 launch from the back of an XB-70 (rather like the Lockheed project to launch a D-21 drone from the back of an SR-71) was briefly considered but not developed.

On March 25, 1967 NASA took sole charge of the XB-70 program, issuing support contracts to NAA and General Electric and expecting to end testing in December 1968. Twenty-two more flights were made. The USAF's TB-58A support continued. The Valkyrie gained NASA

The TB-58A Hustler chase plane usually flew an inside track on the XB-70, staying at lower altitude. One of the Valkyrie pilots invariably occupied the back seat of the Hustler. At Mach 3 (30 miles per minute) the XB-70 took 13 minutes to make a 180-degree turn, covering territory with a 100-mile radius in the process. T-38A chase aircraft took off before the XB-70 and made a 180-degree turn, returning at high speed to keep pace with the Valkyrie as it took off and accelerated to altitude. (NASA)

AV1 in NASA markings completes a landing run with all three brake 'chutes functioning. The aircraft's height above the ground ruled out the normal pre-flight walk-around by the pilot – hand-checking control surfaces, peering up the engine exhausts, and so on. There was a formal, basic walk-around plan, starting at the crew entry ladder and checking 12 areas of the fuselage, wings, landing gear, and intakes, seeing safety pins were in place and so on, but crews were informed that, "Because of the size and complexity of this airplane it is assumed that maintenance personnel have completed the required pre-flight inspections. Information on non-accessible items is listed in the Pre-flight Inspection Record." (NASA)

NAA XB-70A 62-0001
Edwards AFB, California, late 1968

Small identically located acceleration and force vanes were added to either side of the nose by NASA for the aircraft's final ten flights to reduce the effects of turbulence. Rake probes above the wings and fuselage measured boundary layer pressure. NASA's patch appeared on the nose. The wingtips depicted here are in the mid-lowered position at a 25-degree angle.

X PLANES

NAA XB-70A 62-0001, Edwards AFB, California, late 1968

tail logos and it was loaded with additional instrumentation to study gust response, stability, and boundary layer noise. For the final ten flights small rotating vanes were fitted above the wings and to the nose for the Identically Located Acceleration and Force experiment that helped to reduce turbulence.

Fulton and Cotton made the first all-NASA flight on April 25, 1967. By the end of 1968 it had become hard to justify the million dollars per flight that the XB-70 took from shrinking Flight Research Center funds and NASA decided to retire the XB-70 at the same time as the X-15, both of which had contributed greatly to NAA's share of the high-speed test work at Edwards AFB as the world's fastest aircraft. Its 83rd and final flight, a 1,880-mile subsonic trip to Wright-Patterson AFB, Ohio, was only the second time it had left the Edwards AFB area. On February 4, 1969, Fulton and Sturmthal delivered the aircraft to the Air Force Museum at the end of a 3hr 17min structural dynamics test flight and it was put on permanent display.

The Valkyrie was, in Al White's words, "a very remarkable airplane" but he added that it was also "an unfinished airplane" operating in a "completely new speed and altitude range but with off-the-shelf navigation equipment and flight instrumentation that were obsolete for this type of flight operation." He was convinced that, with suitable updates, it would have been "a truly outstanding airplane." Various items were never fully reliable, including the nose-wheel steering and the brakes, which he felt were, at best, "marginally satisfactory." In flight, White found it suffered from "excessive adverse yaw, with a tendency to enter inadvertent sideslips without the pilot's knowledge," requiring the pilot to keep a constant eye on the yaw indicator. Lowering the wingtips to the halfway position reduced this problem.

The XB-70's test flights were seldom straightforward. Chase pilot George Marrett recalled that various technical problems occurred on virtually every flight, and a T-38A crew always had to monitor undercarriage retraction from beneath the XB-70A.

NASA's contribution to high-Mach research is epitomized here by the XB-70 and the hypersonic North American X-15A-2 on August 4, 1967. (NASA via T. Panopalis)

Lt Col Ted Sturmthal made ten XB-70 flights, including its last journey, a ferry flight to the USAF Museum at Dayton, Ohio, as co-pilot with "Fitz" Fulton. (Terry Panopalis collection)

Early in the test program NAA wanted photographs of the aircraft at Mach 1.2 so that the wingtips could be lowered to 65 degrees. The chase/photographic F-104D had to fly ahead of the supersonic shockwave as the aircraft would have become difficult to control if it had been flown within the cone of the shockwave. (NASA)

North American Rockwell, as the company became after September 1967, returned to the bomber business in the 1970s. While hope of reviving the B-70 persisted throughout the early 1960s, the company hoped to develop other possibilities, including a nuclear-powered version with virtually unlimited loiter time. All these hopes were short-lived despite repeated attempts in the Senate to revive the program, and they would not be revitalized until mid-1964 when the USAF issued its requirement for an Advanced Manned Strategic Aircraft. NAA, battling it out with Boeing and General Dynamics once again, received a contract for five supersonic B-1A bombers in June 1970, with the prospect of 240 production examples to follow. Sadly, that prospect too was terminated in 1977 when "stealth" engineering became feasible for a bomber aircraft and only three B-1A prototypes were completed.

Ten years later the surviving Valkyrie was towed into an open-air site outside the Air Force Museum, where it would sit for many years. It was finally housed in the Museum's annex in 2003, where it became an inspiring attraction, the stimulus for many media-world space vehicle designers and a tribute to the ingenuity and massive resources of the US aviation industry.

In October 1970 AV1 was gently maneuvered for eight miles along Route 444 and local roads from Wright-Patterson AFB to its permanent home in the new USAF Museum at Wright Field. The landing gear fitted between the edges of the bridge (left) with a few inches to spare. Most of the internal equipment and the engines had to be removed to reduce the aircraft's weight sufficiently to meet the bridge's structural limits. (USAF)

The route to Wright Field had to be carefully planned to suit the XB-70's size and weight, with many roadside poles and signs having to be moved to allow the Valkyrie through and the aircraft's vertical tails removed to cope with overhead cable obstructions. It stood outside the new museum for 17 years, suffering some damage from skin de-lamination and blistering, before being moved into the Modern Flight Hangar. As the aircraft had officially been returned to USAF custody at the end of the NASA test program, the small vanes above AV1's wings and on its nose had been removed, together with the NASA tail marking, by the time it went on display at the Air Force Museum. During AV1's test program, pilots and ground-operators referred to the aircraft as a "B-70" rather than XB-70. (USAF)

Another hiatus existed until 1981, when President Ronald Reagan took office. He was advised of the secret research that would lead to the Northrop/Boeing B-2A Spirit, but also told that it could not be operational until the mid-1990s. Reagan then agreed to a contract for 100 Mach 1.25-capable B-1B Lancers as another "interim" bomber to supplement the shrinking B-52 force. NAA delivered them to SAC between 1984 and May 1988.

The big, white Valkyrie was overtaken by politics, spiraling costs, and the rapid advances in air defenses. In 1959 Beech Aircraft was anticipating production of its Alert Pod, a turbine-powered support vehicle that would enable SAC's fleet of about 65 B-70s to operate from bases anywhere in the world. It would have provided hydraulic, electrical, and pneumatic power to "quick start" the bomber as it stood on alert status, ready to launch at three minutes' notice (or 20 minutes from a cold start) – it would have been transported to the base below the aircraft's rear fuselage. None were built.

The surviving XB-70, confined to a hangar, shows the windshield arrangement in the lowered position. Before it went on display, the American public had rare glimpses of the Valkyrie in action, beginning with its only flight to a base other than Edwards AFB during the test program. AV2 was flown to the March 1966 Armed Forces Day airshow at Carswell AFB, Texas. In May of that year it made supersonic passes across the crowd at a similar event at Edwards AFB. It was generally assumed that the very public display of the new aircraft at its roll-out and the freedom of information about its capabilities were intended to impress the Russians. Their MiG-25, a response to the threat of high-Mach US bombers, ironically showed that its design had been strongly influenced by NAA's A-5 Vigilante (which was also promoted as a high-altitude interceptor early in its career). Their Sukhoi T-4 was clearly a direct response to the XB-70. (Author's collection)

FURTHER READING

BOOKS

Campbell, John M., *North American XB-70 in Colour* (Schiffer Military History, Atglen, Pennsylvania, 1998)

Campbell, John M. and Pape, Garry R., *North American XB-70 Valkyrie – A Photo Chronicle* (Schiffer Military History, Atglen, Pennsylvania, 1996)

Famous Airplanes Series – No. 106 *XB-70 Valkyrie* (Bunrindo Co Ltd, Tokyo)

Gunston, Bill, *Bombers of the West* (Ian Allan, London, 1973)

Jenkins, Dennis R. and Landis, Tony R., *North American XB-70A Valkyrie* (Warbird Tech Series/Specialty Press, North Branch, Minnesota, 2002)

Jenkins, Dennis R. and Landis, Tony R., *Valkyrie – North American's Mach 3 Superbomber* (Specialty Press, North Branch, Minnesota, 2004)

Kozak, Warren, *LeMay – The Life and Wars of General Curtis LeMay* (Regnery Publishing, Washington, D.C., 2009)

Mallick, Donald M. and Merlin, Peter W., *The Smell of Kerosene – A Test Pilot's Odyssey* (NASA)

Marrett, George J., *Contrails over the Mojave* (Naval Institute Press, Annapolis, Maryland, 2008)

McNamara, Robert S., *Blundering into Disaster – Surviving the First Century of the Nuclear Age* (Pantheon Books, 1986)

McNamara, Robert S., *In Retrospect* (Times Books, New York, 1995)

Pace, Steve, *Valkyrie – North American XB-70* (Aero/TAB Books, Blue Ridge Summit, Pennsylvania, 1990)

Remak, Jennette and Ventolo, Joe, *XB-70 Valkyrie – The Ride to Valhalla* (MBI Publishing Company, Osceola, Wisconsin, 1998)

Simons, Graham M., *Valkyrie – The North American XB-70* (Pen & Sword, Barnsley, 2011)

Slade, Stuart (Ed), *United States Strategic Bombers 1945–2012* (Defense Lion Publications, Newtown, Connecticut, 2012)

DOCUMENTS

A Summary of XB-70 Sonic Boom Signature Data. Maglieri, D. Sothcott, V., and Keefer, T. (NASA, April 1992)

B-70 Standard Aircraft Characteristics (Secretary of the Air Force, June 1960)

Handling Qualities of the XB-70 Airplane in the Landing Approach. Berry, D. and Powers, B. (NASA, February 1970)

Lessons from the XB-70 as Applied to the Supersonic Transport. Fulton, Fitzhugh L. Jr. (NASA 1968)

Preliminary Evaluation of XB-70 Airplane Encounters with High-Altitude Turbulence. Kordes, E. and Love, B. (NASA, October 1967)

Propulsion Flight Research at NAS Dryden from 1967 to 1997. Burcham, F. W., Ray, R. J., Conners, T. R., and Walsh, K. R. (NASA, July 1998)

Statistical Analysis of Landing-Contact Conditions for the XB-70 Airplane. Wilson, R. and Larson, R. (NASA, June 1967)

Summary of XB-70 Airplane Cockpit Environmental Data. Irwin, K. and Andrews, W. (NASA, October 1969)

XB-70A Interim Flight Manual (Secretary of the Air Force, August 1964)

XB-70A Flight Manual Supplement (Secretary of the Air Force, February 1967)

XB-70A Air Vehicle No. 1 Standard Aircraft Characteristics (Secretary of the Air Force, January 1972)

XB-70 Air Vehicle No. 2 Standard Characteristics (Secretary of the Air Force, April 1967)

XB-70 Air Vehicle No. 3 Standard Aircraft Characteristics (Secretary of the Air Force, December 1961)

INDEX